HIGHLAND JOURNEY

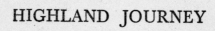

HIGHLAND JOURNEY

or

SÙIL AIR AIS

BY

COLIN MACDONALD

AUTHOR OF "ECHOES OF THE GLEN"

THE MORAY PRESS

EDINBURGH & LONDON

FIRST PUBLISHED SEPTEMBER 1943
REPRINTED SEPTEMBER 1943
„ JULY 1944

PUBLISHED BY THE MORAY PRESS, 21 GEORGE ST., EDINBURGH
AND 29 GT. JAMES ST., BEDFORD ROW, LONDON, W.C. 1

PRINTED BY NEILL AND CO., LTD., EDINBURGH

CONTENTS

PART I

PART II

CHAPTER XIX

CHAPTER XX

CHAPTER XXI

PART III

CHAPTER XXII

CHAPTER XXIII

CHAPTER XXIV

NOTE TO THIRD EDITION

I AM somewhat surprised and altogether delighted by the reception which a varied public has given to *Highland Journey*. In these days of "quotaed" paper it has been found quite impossible to keep up with the demand for it. No doubt there is an element of the truth in what a book-stall friend of mine said when, just prior to the publication of the first edition, she assured me she would order a large number straight away.

"Better not order *too* many," said I. "I wouldn't like to see a pile of unsold copies going stale on your stand."

"Oh," said she, "you needn't be afraid of that. We can sell *anything* these days!"

But indeed—as my lady friend readily admits, and scores of most complimentary letters from readers allege—it would appear that it has sold partly on merit.

Ordinary readers may not notice any alterations in the Gaelic bits in this edition, but Gaelic "purists" no doubt will; and I would have such know that the master hand of my friend Mr Angus MacDonald, Inverness, is responsible. So what? But in any case the main idea is to easily convey the right atmosphere rather than to give a display of irreproachable Gaelic—if such there be!

I have been repeatedly complimented on the Gaelic title "Sùil air Ais (pronounced Sool er ash and meaning "Looking Back"). Now the credit for that really belongs to my friend Dr D. J. MacLeod, O.B.E., to whom, and to Mr MacDonald, I am greatly indebted.

C. M.

PART I

INTRODUCTION

LET me be honest about this book-writing business. Why do I attempt it? For a great statesman, soldier, scientist, scholar, or criminal, writing a book should be an easy matter and a safe venture for his publisher. Such may rest assured of a public intensely interested in his sayings and doings; especially the criminal—if he is a sufficiently notorious criminal. But that a very ordinary fellow like myself should venture to write a book displays a degree of self-assurance, if not of sheer impudence, which—because really I am somewhat of a modest disposition—requires some explanation. Well, in a word, the explanation is the "kick" I get out of it.

Some eight years ago I was—or imagined I was, which is nearly as bad—in a miserable state of health. Work, wife, family, friends, food—all for me had lost flavour. I went about in a state of physical misery and mental perturbation and depression. A serene philosophy which, when in robust health, I had evolved for my guidance and conduct, in whatever circumstances of prosperity or adversity Fate might bring my way, fell to sorry bits at this first test of trouble. That was intensely humiliating. I who had so often in a superior, strong-man sort of way advised others—how they must have hated me!—how to comport themselves under the buffets of Fate, to be so utterly found out. And when it came to the stage that I couldn't laugh at myself I knew the case was serious; that something had to be done about it. I must put a compulsitor on myself: must force myself to take an interest in something.

9

So I wrote to my friend David Watt, of the *Ross-shire Journal*—who indeed *is* the *Ross-shire Journal*—suggesting I should write an article for his paper for each week of 1932. I couldn't give him the foggiest indication of "How the subject theme might gang," but he generously agreed. During that year there appeared each week in the *Ross-shire* an article under the heading *Beachdaireachd* and signed *Beachdair*. These are Gaelic words, the first roughly equivalent to "Stock-taking" and the second meaning "The Fellow who takes Stock." For the first six months the authorship of *Beachdaireachd* was a well-kept secret, and many a time when passing through Dingwall, and some other places in the north, did I join eagerly in local conjecture as to who on earth the author of such interesting articles could be.

Soon a certain tendency in the articles developed. They were prone to browse among my own recollections of early life in a Highland glen; and, as soon appeared, they evoked a keen interest not only locally but in far corners of the world where the *Ross-shire* finds its way to exiled natives of the north. It was then I began to get the "kick" aforementioned. When you are told by an old lady in London—or Australia—of how she cried for joy over some memory-stirring passages you have written, or by an exiled Scot from many places of how he chuckled over certain bits and read them over and over again; and when you get scores of letters in similar strain from a great variety of people at home and abroad, it gives you a grand glow of satisfaction. That was my happy experience, and I who had but a few months before imagined myself past and dead to all human vanity found myself as vain as a peacock: my chest swelling like a pouter pigeon at such tributes to my cleverness. Oh! it was a grand feeling, and more effective than tonics from a dozen doctors.

In 1936 a good deal of *Beachdaireachd* was incorporated

in my *Echoes of the Glen*, whose kindly reception by the Press and public gave me renewed and deeper thrills of that self-conceit a modicum of which, I am convinced, is a most useful, necessary, human attribute. But, mind you, it takes some courage to let a book that you have written go out into the world. For, inevitably, a book is more or less a reflection of its author. To a greater or less degree it lets the critical eye of his friends and fellows penetrate his inmost thoughts and being. Spiritually it is somewhat analogous to what walking along Princes Street without his trousers would be physically. But indeed I was needlessly apprehensive about that, as you will see.

On the morning of the day on which *Echoes of the Glen* was timed to appear in public I was in a fever of self-consciousness. What an ass I had been to write a book at all! It wouldn't catch on! And there was that horrible publicity! I sneaked down in a street car to the Caledonian Station, and in by the side entrance, in agony at the thought of the blatant placards. Timidly I glanced towards the near end of the bookstall, but was surprised and relieved to see no placards there.

"They'll be round at the front," I thought with dismay. So, bravely to the front I went. Not a sign of me or my *Echoes*. I scanned the myriad books on the shelves but nary an *Echo* could I see, nor any reference to it or me. Half-relieved, half-disappointed, I went along Princes Street and glanced at the bookshop windows. Blank again! If it was there I didn't see it.

Somewhat resentful now I made for the Waverley bookstall. "That's where the show will be," thought I.

But the Waverley bookstall was like the other one—oblivious of my existence.

Chuckling now at my previous apprehensions I went to the small bookstall at the east end of the Waverley Station to make sure my child wasn't there. It wasn't in sight, but by bending down and forward and then creaking my neck for an upward glance behind an obscuring shelf I got a shock! There, in its artistic blue-toned cover, was a copy of *Echoes of the Glen*! My heart raced, but I pulled myself together.

With the steadiest voice I could muster, and in most casual manner, I said to the bookstall lady: "I'll take a copy of *Echoes of the Glen*, please," and waited for the brightening of her eye. But there was no brightening: the magic name conveyed nothing to her.

"I beg your pardon?" said the lady.

"*ECHOES of the GLEN*," I repeated distinctly, and in a hopefully suggestive tone.

"Is it a sixpenny one?" the lady brightly inquired.

"No!" I now bawled; "it is a five-shilling one, and it was published this morning."

"Oh, sorry! I haven't got it yet," said the lady, "but maybe you will get a copy at the big bookstall."

"Thank you," I said quite nicely, and I hadn't the heart to tell her that on her shelf there was a copy which she must have put there that morning.

Then and since my experience not only of bookstall assistants, but of booksellers generally—with very rare exceptions—has led me to believe that they take about as much interest in an individual book as a potato merchant takes in an individual potato.

Of the many compliments paid to my initial effort in the book line the one I like perhaps best of all came unconsciously from a Sutherland crofter. Donald was in our Thurso office paying his rent. That formality over, he sat with my colleague, George Stewart, enjoying a pipe and a crack. All of a sudden Donald "remembered" and the following conversation took place:

DONALD. Man, Mister Stewart, did you see that Colin MacDonald has written a book?

G.S. Yes, have you read it?

DONALD. Yes, man, and it's a *grand* book!—there's *nothing* in it!—*anyone* could write a book like yon!—if he could *write* it!

Well, equally there may be "nothing" in this one. I am not even sure that I can write it, but I do venture to hope that of a winter's evening it may give a little entertainment to some of my fellows on the Journey.

CHAPTER I

Shadowy   Glimpses — Long - range   Conversations — Queen's
Jubilee—Stir of the Bagpipes—Cottage and Castle

THE Journey began on 28th January 1882. I was
serenely unconscious of its course for the first year or two.
After that just a spotlight here and there, dimmed almost
immediately to leave but a shadowy memory. There was,
for instance, that day I saw at the foot of the bed a strange
man, wearing black whiskers and a black suit, carrying a
black bag in his hand. I saw him shake his head and
heard him speak to my mother, who looked unhappy.
Years later I learned that he told her there was only a
faint hope of my pulling through. I also learned that
within ten days I was doing full justice to porridge and
potatoes and herrings again.

Then a little later there was the time my father surprised
us. Like every self-respecting Highland crofter of his day
he left the performance of all domestic duties to his women-
folk. I had never seen him sweep the house floor, cook a
meal (other than stir his own brose), milk a cow, or "wait"
on us children in his life. Imagine my surprise then when
one morning he came to the kitchen bed, where three of us
were lying, carrying a tray with plates of porridge for us!
The reason for this astounding phenomenon was a double
one: we three were recovering from measles, and the
previous night my youngest sister had been born. But I
cannot remember him lapsing to that extent on any future
occasion.

About the age of three I remember sitting on a stool on
a table near the window of a maiden aunt's house trying
to catch flies, that crawled across the panes, and hoping to
put them into a *pocan-ordaig* (a thumb-screwed paper bag).

It was a day of disappointments: the flies just slid away before my fingers could get them.

Four or so saw—and heard—me exchanging greetings by shouting to the wife of our nearest neighbour two hundred yards away. I have frequently seen townspeople amazed at the facility with which country folks can carry on a conversation with neighbours at anything up to a mile. In this art, as in most others, early training counts for much. The star performer in our district was the Griasaich Mòr (Big Shoemaker). Once on a still, frosty May morning, while an uncle and myself were metalling the road at Contin Bridge, we heard the Griasaich as clear as a bell calling on his dog "Curly." The distance by bee-line from the Griasaich's house to Contin Bridge is just over three miles.

In 1887 came Queen Victoria's Jubilee celebrations. There is more substance in this memory. Every bairn in the district went, with a mug, to the Castle Park. There were races, in which all competitors were prize-winners, some dancing, and—the first I had ever seen—a gigantic piper majestically arrayed in all the gaudy trappings of his trade. That piper fascinated me and my coevals, and soon after some of the older boys got practising chanters. In the afternoon we all marched into the Castle, to be regaled on pie and lemonade—another novelty to most of us. Not even champagne in after years quite touched the glory of that first lemonade— which was contained in yon old bottles with rounded bottoms like Indian clubs.

The Castle was awesome, as were the folks who lived in it. Its high, grim, six-foot-thick walls, its richly furnished wood-floored rooms, were such a contrast to our own thatch-roofed, earth-floored little houses. Seeing the Castle at close quarters for the first time gave me my first twinge of inferiority. Later in life, a fairly extensive

familiarity with castles and those who live in them led me
to the knowledge that the latter, in the things that really
matter, are not so different or superior after all.   I have
quite ceased either to fear or envy them.   If anything, I
rather pity them.   Of this I am certain : that if freedom
from worry and debts and pretence—that awful blight on
human life—and the possession of robust health and loving,
happy, family unity be applied as the measure of a
desirable existence, then the average inhabitant of the
crofter's cottage leaves the average inhabitant of the castle
far behind.

CHAPTER II

Lament for the Linnet—School Elements—Youthful Naturalists—
The New Headmaster

SCHOOL came at five. In *Echoes of the Glen* I tried to give
a few glimpses of our doings there, so I must avoid repeti-
tion, but will venture a few further references to our rural
academy. The school lay in the flat of the valley, some
five hundred feet lower than our home. Of my first day
of book-learning I retain only one, but most vivid memory.
All the bairns from higher up "The Heights" called for
us on their way to school that morning to give convoy to
the new scholar. There were three of the gamekeeper's
family from far up the hill-side, two cousins from just
above us, and three of our nearest neighbour's bairns.
Lower down we collected the MacKays, and when we
came to the railway crossing we were joined by a bigger
contingent from the Bottacks. Of course, I was the show-
piece, and very shy and embarrassed I felt by the crowd's
attentions. Instead of crying—as I very nearly did—I
picked up a stone from the railway and threw it as far as
I could along the line. It was a sort of gesture of independent manliness which I was far from feeling. Speak
of "shots at random sent"! That stone happened to
come bang down on the steel rail, about ten yards away,
a fraction of a second after a young linnet had alighted at
that identical spot. It was instant death to the linnet.
The bigger boys were impressed by such marksmanship:
what an eye! what an aim! I felt momentarily proud of
a feat which—quite undeservedly—jumped my stock
in the market of that somewhat callous lot of hooligans'
esteem; but indeed my triumph held a cankerous seed,
for, as I looked at that pathetic fluffy little heap, still

warm and trembling, which but moments before had been the incarnation of joy and gladness, a tear rolled down my nose and I had to laugh in raucous bravado to avoid disgrace. That little linnet remains the only song-bird I have injured in my life; and when at the last bar of judgment I shall be asked, as I still dread—"Why did you do it?"—the only plea I can tender is that I didn't mean it and that it has been a lifelong regret.

There were over a hundred scholars all told, with a headmaster, a headmistress, and two pupil teachers to instruct them. The scholars came from four main social strata. An outsider might well fail to see reason for differentiation, but he would be wrong. In numerical order we derived from:

1. *The farm-servant class.*—A prolific breed: I remember one family of fourteen, two of twelve each, two of nine, one of eight, and one of seven—a total of seventy-one, which assured an average school contingent of about two dozen—at one farm alone. With the individual family wage totalling not more than from twenty-five to thirty pounds per annum, plus an allowance of meal, milk, potatoes, and coal, one may assume that pampering in their early years did not spoil the family of the farm servant. Only God and their mothers knew how they were clothed and fed. But they were a tough and hardy race, who in the main took to hard manual labour—what other choice had they?—as soon as the attainment of their fourteenth birthday freed them from compulsory attendance at school. With few exceptions—but I can think of some bright ones—they were below the average in scholastic attainments; but that was probably largely due to their parents' nomadic propensity, which gave them little opportunity of a continuous course of education at one school.

2. *The crofting community.*—The "Heighters," as we

were called, lived up on the braes, where their progenitors had lived in the same croft for generations—in some cases centuries. Here was greater solidity and permanence; also a good deal more of material and cultural advantages which such permanence engenders. But we were still far, far, from being pampered! Almost invariably it was from this section the school's best scholars came. There was a second crofter contingent who came from the adjacent parallel valley, where their parents or grand-parents, on being evicted from the estate of another land-lord, had been permitted by our landlord to settle on small areas of unreclaimed land, which they industriously brought into cultivation. These still lacked the homo-geneity of the older community; but they were a friendly, hospitable people, known—a reference to their original home—as the *Cononachs*.

3. *Villagers' families.* — Shopkeepers, feuars, estate officials, etc., a comparatively well-to-do class. These youngsters esteemed themselves no small beer, and infinitely superior to the "Heighters" and the farm "Sgalags," whom they held in supreme contempt. It is only fair to say, though, that we returned this unchart-able sentiment with interest. There was a satisfying savour of opprobrium in the nickname of "Strath Scraabs" which we used to hurl at them in our after-school-hours battles.

4. *Farmers' families.*—A very small contingent indeed: mostly such didn't come to our school at all. Their parents had more ambitious and (?) better views in regard to the education of their offspring.

The school classes were simple and obvious in their progression:

The First Book, Penny Book, or A, B, C.

The Second Book (2*d*.).

The Third Book (3*d*.).

Standard I.
Standard II.
Standard III.
Standard IV.
Standard V.
Standard VI.
Ex-VI Standard.

Even if you waited at school to take the "Ex-sixth" you should finish at fourteen: but if you were unfortunate enough to finish with the Ex-sixth at twelve—as some of us did—unless your parents could afford to send you to another school you had no alternative but go on, like a repeating decimal, on that same standard till at fourteen you earned emancipation. This repeating business was, I am sure, largely responsible for the reign of rebellion against discipline which for years was rank in our school. The older boys *had* to do something interesting. As they couldn't very well continue to be interested in the same dry lessons year after year they resorted to many ingenious trouble-making devices, which gave spice and variety to their period of compulsory detention—and incidentally did much to whiten the beard of the headmaster.

The assortment of natural-history specimens which a group of industrious country boys could collect during the midday play-hour was surprising. Half a dozen paddocks from the marsh near the mill-dam, a dozen eels from the mill-lade, a match-box full of bees—bumbees, *boddach ruadhs*, and *ton-deargans*—mice, *fiolagans*, and an occasional rat were a reasonable expectation. And you have no idea how this menagerie, stealthily liberated at various places on the classroom floor, could make the dominie hop and splutter with rage. And when, as sometimes happened, in process of shooing the creatures out of doors or windows, "himself" was well stung by a wasp, did we howl! Of course, it was fiendishly wicked! But there you were! We enjoyed it, and if some of us—often the wrong ones—paid the penalty in pandies and by being "kept in" it was still worth it.

That poor man! Yet looking back I am convinced it was largely his own fault. No one who cannot control his—or her—own temper need ever hope to control a class of boys. Neither can he hope to win their confidence or respect. The opposite was strikingly proved in this small school some years after my time. The old dominie was followed by a succession of female "heads," who took the very earliest opportunity of resigning. At last a man was appointed. He was rumoured to be one who would soon have the rebels (now riotously triumphant) in subjection. The big boys held an anxious conclave to decide on measures adequate for putting the new master in his place and so ensure continuance of "freedom." "Fireworks" were timed to begin in the forenoon of the very first day. But the new master forestalled them. He made an opening speech to the rebels—something to this effect—and he spoke throughout in a friendly, chummy tone, but with a deadly disconcerting ring at the back of it:

"Well, lads, here I am, the new master of this school. I hear that you have your own views about that: that *you* have been in the habit of bossing the school and that you mean to continue to do so. Well, as I mean to be boss—that's partly what I'm paid for—it looks as if there might be a spot of trouble unless—and I'll make a sporting offer—unless we can come to a friendly understanding. I have here" (he produced a vicious-looking belt) "a strap which, if I must, I will use freely and forcefully to get that discipline without which no school can be of much use. On the other hand, if you give me your word of honour that you will obey my orders—and I promise they will be fair and reasonable—that strap goes into this drawer, and will remain there while I am headmaster here. The choice is yours. You can now go to the playground for half an hour to talk the matter over amongst yourselves. At the end of the half-hour I will ring you in and get your decision as to whether it is to be peace or war."

They went out. This method of challenge was highly disconcerting. Even "Fraochie," who was one of the riot ringleaders, counselled peace.

"Ach! Shut up! Who's going to be a softie," insisted "Binks," "doing everything you're told like a baby!"

Each got some backing, but the weight of opinion was with Fraochie. The bell summoned them in with the great question still undecided.

"Well," said the new dominie, "what is the verdict?"

No answer: only an embarrassed silence.

"In that case," the head announced, "we will just go on with the day's work and see what happens."

He hadn't long to wait. Binks the bellicose would not be disgraced: he had a reputation to maintain. He shouted to someone in the front seat inquiring if his mother knew he was out, or some such witticism.

"Binks," said the new master quietly, and without a trace of anger (and fancy him knowing the nickname, and using it!), "if you do that sort of thing again I shall punish you good and hard."

A direct challenge! That was enough: Binks bawled some other inanity at a front-bencher. But he had no intention of being caught. In former days when he wanted to elude a walloping one stratagem was to run along the back seat away from the centre corridor, thereby encouraging pursuit, and when he got the old dominie well messed up among the desks he made a bee-line over the top of them for the door and freedom. It nearly succeeded this time. But the new dominie had played

Rugby. With a low tackle he downed Binks near the door. The mutineer's strength was as straw to the steel of this man's muscles. The next few minutes for Binks were a painful experience. It was an all-in devastating loundering that not even Binks—and I would never decry his pluck—could continue to stand up to. At the first howl for mercy the dominie stopped, still smiling if somewhat grim.

"Sorry, Binks! I had to keep my promise," he said really quite kindly. "Will we shake hands and be friends for the future?"

It was a bitter pill, but Binks had savvy to see in which way lay wisdom. They shook hands, and to Binks' credit he scrupulously observed the compact. Ceremoniously, the belt was consigned to the drawer, where it lay undisturbed and unrequired throughout the years of that dominie's reign.

CHAPTER III

First Love—Timing the Tank—Blasted Romance

THERE was a lassie who came to school the same year as myself. Right through the school years we had sat side by side in class. Her hair was abundant and wavy and brown. Her grey-blue eyes were so warm and kind. Her cheeks were suffused with that so adorable rosy blush of rural health. And her lovely rounded soft-firm throat and neck disappeared so intriguingly beneath a white blouse! And she was so quiet and kind in her voice and ways. She usually sat on my left, so that, when the afternoon sun shone in at the window—as it often did—it glorified her hair and face and whole expression in a way that thrilled to my inmost being. This my first was a lustless love: a pure, tender emotion. Old folks should never laugh at calf-love. It is indeed something pure and sacred, which usually finds its only expression in little acts of service. On one occasion it inspired me to real heights of altruism. It was during the annual competition for the dux medal. All forenoon the competitors had wrestled with history, geography, and "sums," as we called arithmetic. There was one of those tricky problems where a tank of given length, depth, and breadth is being fed by water from a tap of certain diameter and emptied through another tap of lesser calibre. Given an empty tank and the two taps set to functioning at full bore you have to calculate how long it will take the tank to reach the overflow point. I have often thought how much more easily and pleasantly most youngsters could solve such problems with actual tanks and taps and a watch. But of course that would eliminate those exercises in mental gymnastics which arithmetic is designed to provide.

Anyhow, to some at our school the elucidation of such problems via slate and pencil processes remained for ever a profound mystery. You are just born with a gift that way, or without. I happened to be in the former category. Mary—that wasn't her name, but it will serve—wasn't. At the play-hour I asked her how she had got on with the tank sum. She hadn't. She hadn't been able even to make a shape at it. Tear-drops trembled in those kind eyes. I just couldn't stand it.

"Go," I said, "round to the back of the west dyke and wait there till I come."

She went. I collected a bit of broken slate, hid it under my jacket, and stole round to where she was waiting. In five minutes I had figured out on the slate the solution of the mystery of the tank. In less than other five minutes she had copied it out on a piece of paper for afternoon use—thereby jeopardising my chance of winning the medal. I still rate that as the most gallant action of my life.

School finished, Mary went her way; I went mine. For over forty years we never met. Indeed, we lost all trace of each other. But even to an oldish family man there sometimes came a tender memory of a schoolgirl sweetheart.

A few years ago, back in the homeland I entered a local ladies' emporium to exchange greetings with the proprietrix. I found her engaged with a customer and offered to withdraw.

"Don't go," said the lady of the shop; "you two surely know each other? Why, you must have been at school together!"

I looked at a *cailleach* of ample form and white hair and many wrinkles—an utter stranger. She looked at my waistless form and hairless dome. Not a jot of recognition on either side.

"Goodness me! Weren't you in school with Mary ——, and weren't you in school with Colin MacDonald?" inquired the shopkeeper.

"Mary!" I gasped; but believe me there was tender emotion in my voice and a warm feeling at the heart of me. For me, as by magic, the *cailleach* was transformed into a lassie of twelve with sunlit hair and grey kind eyes. Indeed, I was deeply moved, and I looked for similar glad response. But I looked in vain! Not a vestige of recollection: not even of my name!

"But surely, surely, you can't have forgotten *me*?" I said, incredulous.

But no! At first I thought so utter a memory-blank could not be possible. But soon I knew it was no pretence. She just couldn't place me, or at least but vaguely. It was indeed a tragi-comical ending to an exquisite memory that had remained with me off and on for nearly half a century.

But, still, I repeat: old folks should not ridicule a thing so pure and sacred as the first love of a laddie.

CHAPTER IV

The Whupper-in—Storks and Angels—First Earnings—Rory's
"Rosie"—'A' Bhò Ruadh (Red Cow)

WHILE there was never any suggestion of lack of the
essentials of life in our circles, coin of the realm was a
rarity. Augmentation of the family funds, therefore, was
the concern of everyone, including youngsters down to
seven or so. In this connection, compulsory attendance
at school—a recent innovation—was somewhat of a
trouble. But there was a sensible leniency in regard to
the matter during summer and autumn, when most
opportunities of getting a money-making job occurred.
Then old Daanie the "Whupper-in" postponed his
admonitory visit as long as his fairly accommodating
conscience permitted. Considerable reflection on this
point has led me to the conclusion that those latter-day
educationists who make a fetish of "regular attendance"
and regard "child labour" as a crime might well take a
leaf out of Daanie's book—with advantage to all concerned.

At a very early age most of us were skilled in a variety
of jobs. The boys knew exactly how much straw or hay
or turnips should be given to the different beasts—including variations near foaling or calving—and were trusted
to feed them accordingly; and there is much more in
that than most people who don't know imagine.

Because of our smaller hands we could in difficult cases
give more effective help than our parents to a lambing
ewe or calving cow—and were occasionally called upon
to do so. For us there were no storks or angels about
births or deaths: just an intelligent understanding and
sensible acceptance of natural happenings.

Singling turnips; turning, gathering, and coling hay;

planting and lifting potatoes; lifting and binding corn, and setting it up in stooks ("Set end-wise to twelve o'clock of the sun and don't you forget it!"); forking, building cart-loads of sheaves; threshing and winnowing grain, and many other operations requiring a surprising degree of skill were all well within the compass of boys— ay, and most girls too—before they reached their teens; and already the boys would be ambitious to try their hand at ploughing, sowing, drilling, building stacks ("Keep your stack well hearted-up in the centre, man, or your sheaves will take in the rain instead of throwing it out!"), and some of the more highly skilled—almost sacred— agricultural arts.

One of my first wage-earning jobs did not encroach on school hours. It started when I was eight, and I had three seasons of it. Certain crofts were too small to provide summer grazing for the family cow. In such cases the cows were sent to graze on the cow-park near the Castle. They had to be driven there each morning and home each night. I took on the contract of driving three. A neighbouring lassie aged eleven was responsible for another couple of cows, and we made one drove of the lot. At seven-thirty each morning for four months (bar Sundays, when the cows were tethered at home) I called for Rory Ruadh's cow "Rosie," then for Aunty Maggie's "Daisy," and finally for Anna Nic Aoinish's nameless old brown cow.

In addition to cash wages (five shillings per cow per season) there were unspecified but never-failing perquisites to the drover. From Rory's grown-up daughter there was a "piece" of loaf bread with butter and honey. Aunty Maggie (who had a shoppie) gave a handful of "lozengers" or "bachelor-buttons" or a caraway-seed biscuit. Anna was old, and went back to bed after doing the morning milking, but never failed to leave a *ceapaire*

—oatcake, butter, crowdie, *and* jam—on top of the garden gate-post. All was grist to my anatomical mill, and went the same road as did my regular breakfast of porridge and cream on my return home at nine o'clock preparatory to starting off for school.

Driving the "empty" cows in the morning was a short and simple job. Driving them home at night with their bellies blown to bursting-point compelled a canny, stately pace calling for philosophic patience, and woe betide if Rory's Rosie arrived in a state of distressful peching!

Was I proud that late September day going home with my first fifteen shillings? And did my health or education suffer?

We of the crofts did not regard our live stock merely as commercial possessions to be ruthlessly bartered for gain. True, we did sell off each year the lambs and stirks and an occasional foal; but these had not yet attained to that degree of warm affection with which we regarded the permanent stock. *Bhò Ruadh* (Red Cow) and *Bhò Bhan* (White Cow) and Maggie-the-Mare were more or less members of the family, all doing their utmost for the common good. Consequently, when Anno Domini did at last compel a severance with one of these, there was gloom in the household for several days. In the case of *Bhò Ruadh* this distress was intensified, as you will see.

Bhò Ruadh had been on the place years before I was born. She was a strawberry-red, always as lean as one of Pharaoh's dream cows, but with the silken skin which denotes good health and the heavy milker. Not once in her fifteen years of maturity had she failed to contribute a calf to the family wealth each spring. But alas! though she still retained much of youthful appearance, prudence advised getting rid of her. One day I overheard my father say to my mother he was afraid *Bhò Ruadh* would have to be sold.

They were speaking in the Gaelic, but fine I understood what they were saying, and I think that was the first big sadness in my life. *Bhò Ruadh* to be sold! *Bhò Ruadh* that was there before I could remember! The cow I had so often herded on the good belts of grass that grew at the edges of the corn and turnip fields! Truth to tell, I didn't like the herding. What a wearisome job it was to have to stand by for hours and hours watching that the beasts didn't steal a turnip or a mouthful of oats. Herding was the bane of my young life. Even now I protest herding is a job for old, old men—not for active boys.

Yet herding had some compensations too. There was ample time for observing the queer ways of the bird and insect life that swarmed around. Blackies, Mavies, *Buidheags*, Binkies; grasshoppers with their ticking noises but so difficult to locate; *Corra-chòsags* (Slaters) that lay under flat stones, and *Sneamhans* and *Gobhlachans* (ants and forky-tails) and Jennies-with-the-hundred-feet, and a thousand other queer and interesting creatures.

Often indeed, on beasties bent, the main job was forgotten until a warning shout from a watchful parent brought us sharply to earth, and the knowledge that the cows, like those of Boy Blue, were in the corn!

There was also the fascination of watching the cows feeding. Yon long tongue would come out and coil itself round a bit of grass to be cut against the upper lip and taken into the mouth and swallowed without chewing at all!

And when the cows had taken so much that their sides bulged like balloons I would drive them in the gloaming back into the byre. Then Mother would come with a *creaban* (milking-stool) and pail, and hum a Gaelic air that set *Bhò Ruadh* to chewing her cud, as with strong and practised fingers the jets of milk were squirted into the pail so that a crown of froth was formed that rose and rose and looked like spilling over, but never did.

Near the end of the milking Mother would take from me my jug. This she filled with the last jets of milk— "strippings"—that were so rich in cream, and I would drink it off at one go. That was the stuff to make a man of a fellow!

These—or something like these—were the thoughts which went vaguely through my mind as I thought with sorrow in my heart of *Bhò Ruadh* being taken to the market and sold to a stranger!

When the dreadful day arrived, Mother and myself went down with Father and *Bhò Ruadh* as far as the county road. They went on. We came back, and indeed there was a load of sorrow on the heart of both.

"Och! *Bhò Ruadh* was getting old anyway," said Mother, trying to comfort herself as well as me. "And *Seonaid* will make a fine cow. Besides," she added, "Father will not sell *Bhò Ruadh* to any drover that comes along. He will try to get her a good home even if he has to take less money for her."

But indeed it was sore hearts we had all the same.

We had a busy day though. We shifted *Seonaid* into *Bhò Ruadh's* stall. We also shifted *Mairi*—that was a young sister of *Seonaid*—from the calf-pen into *Seonaid's* old stall, so that when *Seonaid's* calf came there would be a place for it in the pen.

Then when my father came home from the market and showed us the eight golden sovereigns he had got for *Bhò Ruadh*, and we thought of the many useful things these would buy, we nearly forgot our grief. We were delighted to learn, too, that *Bhò Ruadh* had been sold to a gamekeeper, who lived in a glen over twenty miles away, where she was sure to be well fed and well treated.

To get to her new home *Bhò Ruadh* had to travel

some fifteen miles by train and thence some ten miles by road up the glen.

"She will be arriving at her new home just about now," said Father, looking at the old wag-at-the-wa' before we went to bed about ten o'clock.

But it was some time before I slept. *Bhò Ruadh* and recollections of her would come into my mind, and I'm not saying but there was a damp spot on my pillow that night.

Moreover, when sleep did come it was disturbed by crazy dreams in which *Bhò Ruadh* shed copious tears and then howled like a dog.

Suddenly I realised that it was morning and that there *were* some queer noises going on. The first distinct noise I heard was Rover barking furiously.

"Quiet! Rover," commanded my father from his bed. But not a quiet would Rover. He barked and louder barked in the kitchen.

"What on earth is the matter with that dog?" I could hear my mother say.

Then the strangest thing happened.

"Moo—amoo—amoo!" bellowed a cow outside.

"Gracious me!" exclaimed Mother. "If *Bhò Ruadh* wasn't in Fannich I would say that was her *geimnich* (lowing). But of course it can't be her."

"No, of course it can't," said Father. "*Bhò Ruadh* was never a mile away from here in her life until yesterday, when she was carried fifteen miles away in a train and then walked a further ten miles to Fannich. It can't possibly be *Bhò Ruadh*. It will be one of the shoemaker's cows broken loose."

"Moo—amoo—amoo!" came the strident call again. In a moment I was at the door in my bare feet.

"It's *Bhò Ruadh* right enough!" I yelled. "And there she is standing at the byre door waiting to be milked!"

And sure enough *Bhò Ruadh* it was, footsore and weary with her twenty-five-mile overnight tramp. There was a look half of bovine content and half of reproach in her large brown eyes.

But och! she was glad to be home!

CHAPTER V

Down at the Castle grounds a wealthy shooting tenant
would spend in five months in rearing pheasants more
money than was required to feed and clothe the whole of
the bairns in the neighbourhood for five years. The
process involved the importation of bags of ants—a great
big black crawly variety—that kept together in a heap
round the base of the trunk of a tree until gradually
removed in pailfuls to feed the pheasant chicks. The aim
and purpose of the whole thing was to provide maybe a
fortnight's sport to half a dozen "gents." It seemed—
and seems—a frightful waste of money; yet it is mightily
difficult to say just when money is wasted. Anyhow even
the pheasant-rearing had its compensations for us:

(1) We supplied the clocken hens—at twice the price
we could have got otherwise—and got them back for
nothing at the end of the season if they still survived.

(2) One or two boys from the crofts got a job assisting
at the rearing.

(3) Every man and lad in the district who could go
got a few days at the "beating" at good pay.

(4) There was a goodish remnant of the pheasants
which spread over the crofts, and if occasionally a cock
put his foot in a snare meant for a rabbit, how could we
help that?

My brother at the age of twelve was one of the assistants
at the rearing, earning ten shillings per week. One
memorable week, when for some reason he was off duty,
I deputised and got seven-and-sixpence for myself. I
felt oppressed with affluence.

In November and December, in the year of a late harvest, the grouse if left undisturbed would play havoc with the stooks on the higher lying crofts. One such year they came to Kenny Fair's and Rory Choinnich's stooks in hundreds, and I earned a whole pound in one month scaring them off. "Earned" is the right word too. I had to be on the spot before the streak of dawn, wait there for a couple of hours till the people of the croft were themselves free to shoo them away, and then back again from early gloaming till dark. The tedium of this job was greatly relieved by an old muzzle-loading gun into which I packed powder to blaze away with terrific noise.

One winter my brother had a rabbit-killing contract on the estate—threepence per couple. It wasn't too bad either, on the whole. Ten couples per day meant half-a-crown—then big pay for a lad of fourteen. Snares, traps, ferrets, and nets were the stock-in-trade. Occasionally, on a Saturday, I went to give a hand. One such day in December I won't soon forget. It was one of those hard frosty days with a biting north-east wind and feathering snow. The hard ground put traps and snares out of the question; so off we set with two ferrets — one borrowed from a neighbour whose most cherished possession it was.

We decided to try the holes above Glen Sgaich, some two miles from home. Within seconds of putting a ferret in the first hole a grand bunny was in the bag. A good start. It was going to be a record day! But then things began to go wrong. The ferret "stuck." We could hear unmistakable sounds of a kill inside. Botheration! The brute would drink his fill of his victim's blood and then sleep for hours in the warmth of its body; and it was Duncan's precious ferret, that we must not lose nor leave!

We resorted to all the known expedients: we thudded the earth with our feet; we made mouth-noises like a squealing rabbit; we rattled the dead rabbit in the mouth of the hole; we gutted it and proffered the entrails as an enticement; we put in the other ferret (muzzled), but divil a nose did that precious ferret of Duncan's show.

Snow had started to fall at midday. It was already forming considerable drifts. The cold penetrated to our very hearts. We rubbed our ears, we slapped our arms, we danced; but there was a deadly persistence in the increasing cold. Finally, with darkness coming on, we built the ferret-box into the mouth of the hole so that (we hoped) the ferret could not escape, and when his orgy was over would probably sleep in the box, where he might be found next morning. The last bite of our "piece" had been consumed by three o'clock. We were terribly hungry. By now the snowdrifts were so deep that the direct line across the moor was dangerous. The long way round was the quick way home, so we trudged down to the railway and along its weary length. The final lap was up a steep brae through fields, and snow that in places lay ten feet deep. But for Alick's example of sheer pluck I would have lain down and perished. As it was, of the last half-mile I never had but a vague recollection, but I did remember falling in at the door and thinking grimly that that one rabbit represented a hard-earned three-halfpence.

Johnnie MacLeod was one of the drovers who visited the crofts periodically to try to buy stirks, pigs, calves, or other live stock on which to turn a profit. Johnnie was rather a favourite. He never tried to do us down too badly and sometimes, when old women were the sellers, he was known to give more than market value. One week in July Johnnie bought seven pigs in the neighbourhood. He asked Jockie (my cousin) and myself if we would drive the pigs to Dingwall—to arrive at eleven o'clock on the Wednesday forenoon—for which service he offered us two shillings apiece. That was good going! We agreed. But we could not claim much experience in driving pigs. Johnnie said we would learn. He was right. Our deficiency was to be amply remedied on the Wednesday!

First, there were the contests with individual pigs while we were in process of getting them together. When at last they were in one lot it was soon obvious they were not of one mind. Certain bitter animosities were immediately discernible. For example, the tailor's pig—a cannon-snouted ugly enough looking brute himself—conceived a violent dislike—nay, hatred—for "Bogaran's" snub-nosed inoffensive-looking little porker. Straightway Cannon-snout bit a gash out of Snub-nose's neck. The latter emitted a piercing squeal which might have satisfied the former as to which was the boss. But it only encouraged him. He next attacked in flank, then in the rear, and then all round, till his poor victim was streaming gore on all sides. We did our best with admonitory hazel switches, but a pig bent on bullying is not easily dissuaded. We had just decided we must separate the two if Bogaran's pig was to reach Dingwall alive—when there was a dramatic change. Presumably Snub-nose decided if he were to die anyway he would die game. A red light showed in his beady eye. The worm turned. With the courage of despair he made a grab at the tender area beneath his tormentor's tail and hung on. For a moment the bully didn't believe; but soon the reality of the situation was painfully borne in on him. Bully that he was, he squealed at the first hurt. He set off full gallop down the road—fortunately in the right direction—with Bogaran's little hero clinging to his rear. We laughed till we nearly cried.

There were several minor conflicts between other members of our drove, and between them all and us as to the road to be travelled; but Cannon-snout *v.* Snub-nose remained the star turn till we reached the railway bridge. There, right below the bridge, there was a dark shadow due to the brightly shining sun. As by one accord the pigs came to a dead halt. We shooed them and shoved them and switched them in vain. Divil a pig would set foot on the black shadow. While we were still arguing the matter out what should come along but a goods train. More than once since then I have deliberately tried to stand under that iron bridge while a train thundered overhead. Believe me, it takes a deal of nerve. On our charges the result was terrific. Two jumped forward and disappeared round the bend. The other five bounded back, with noses to the ground and tails in the air. Two of them barged through the hedge into a field of standing barley on the left. Another jumped a wooden gate on the right, while the remaining two scorched back for home as if seven devils were after them as well as in them.

To describe how we got our stampeded swine together again, and finally into Dingwall, only half an hour behind scheduled time, would be too painful even after the lapse of half a century. It must suffice to say that get them in we did, and that the two shillings reward did not seem so generous as when we so blithely took on the contract.

CHAPTER VI

Nearly a Minister — Providential Intervention — Freedom — Disillusionment—Literary Relief—Agricultural Lights—Ignoramus

AT thirteen I had already done two years in the ex-sixth standard. As a further year's attendance at school was still necessary, and as the family finances would not stand the strain of sending me to a Higher Grade school, it was decided that during the next year the old dominie would give me special tuition in subjects which, in consultation with my parents, he thought might lay a useful foundation in learning for one destined for the Church—which holy career they had decided I should follow. The choice of subjects showed worldly common sense: Greek, Latin, Agriculture, and Accountancy were the selection. A sixpenny text-book in each of these subjects was duly procured and I was to start in immediately after the annual School Inspection in March. But never a lesson out of these books did I ever learn. It would almost seem that a watchful Providence, concerned for the reputation of the Church, decided to intervene. Anyhow, what did happen was this.

The day of the Inspection came on wild and stormy. By night there was a gale blowing. During the day, my father, concerned for the newly thatched barn-roof, had laid a wooden slab horizontally on top of the thatch. To keep weight on the slab he set up a long ladder so as to lie on top of it, and to keep weight on the ladder he rested a heavy granite boulder a few rungs from the ground. He and I went to do "the eight o'clock" —*i.e.* supper the beasts and see them all right for the night. We had to carry *muileans* of straw from the barn to the byre. The lantern blew out in the gale. In the pitch-darkness I stumbled over the bottom of the ladder. My hands went to the ground; the big stone shook from its place and fell on my left hand. When we got back into the barn it was seen that half a forefinger was gone and its neighbour crushed to a pulp.

I never went back to school. By the time the damaged hand had recovered, my father was down with pneumonia and I, at the age of thirteen and a half, put down that year's turnip crop—dunging, drilling, sowing, and all— quite the proudest youth in Scotland.

What a joy to be free of school and those confounded lessons that didn't seem to lead anywhere! And, when you come to think of it, if pleasure and pride in personal achievement are eliminated it makes the world a dreary place for all but folks of the butterfly type, who are content if they contrive to get what they call "a good time" without doing anything to earn it. Fine I mind the thrill it gave me as I rested the horses for a breather and looked critically at the ploughed rig. There were the furrows—*sgrioban*, we called them—as like each other as the ribs in corduroy, straight and true and well packed, with not a blade of grass showing above. What a perfect bed for the seed that would be soon scattered on it.

And the sowing itself! Who that was ever a two-handed sower can forget yon lovely April morning when the seed-bags stood like sentinels along the ploughed field that was emerald-bordered by the new-coming grass? When the lea was in good fettle and the larks sang riotously overhead? And the seed-box was replenished by a bonnie lassie? And when he himself stepped out so grandly, with a swish and a swing of the arms, to arch the handful of grain like a rainbow so that it fell with a patter which to the attuned and practised ear gave the assurance of uniformity?—who, I say, that was ever a sower can ever forget that poem of a morning or his delight in his own achievement?

That mood lasted for three years. Then one morning, as I was spreading dung in the potato drills, all clarted up with mud and filth, didn't my cousin pass my way *en route* for the town office where he had found employment. Somehow I had never particularly noticed before, but that morning, as I looked at his beautifully creased trousers, polished shoes, dickey and tie AND kid gloves, a first glimpse of realities came to me. Good gosh! Here was I, mud to the knees of my moleskin trousers, spreading dung and planting potatoes, with not a glint of a hope of anything better in all my life.

After Jockie passed on I sat on the dyke for quite a while thinking out the whole position. That was a bitter morning. A lump as of lead seemed to press on my heart —and more or less remained there for three or four years. A dull aching pain, with a terrible longing for a way out; but never a ray of hope.

The chief solace in these awful years of bitter thoughts and frustration was reading. In the little hall we had built for our social evenings was a Library presented by Andrew Carnegie—the Dunfermline boy who had become America's Steel King. There was a good selection— Scott, Dickens, Thackeray, Burns, Biography, Travel— 600 volumes in all. What a revel! I read practically all of them, and many of them many times over. There were also some battered volumes of an early edition of the *Encyclopædia Britannica* (with the old "ʃ" for "s"), which proved a veritable mine of delight.

There was the further delight of debate during our winter sessions. Not infrequently, one of the next week's leaders in debate would come and ask me to give him a hand with his paper—for the affirmative side. Then the leader for the negative would come with a similar request.

With the greatest pleasure I undertook both commissions, and on the night of the debate would speak in support of what appeared to be the weaker side.

Another godsend was the "night class" started one winter by the new schoolmaster when I was about twenty. In two winters there I learned more than I had learned in my eight years at ordinary school.

Then there was another interesting development. In my capacity of secretary of our Literary Society, I one day received a letter from a man who signed himself "George G. Esslemont." The letter was headed : "Aberdeen and North of Scotland College of Agriculture." Mr Esslemont asked if he might have the use of our hall for a series of lectures on agriculture. The request seemed to me to be a queer one. What on earth could anyone lecture about on agriculture? Surely we knew all that was to be known about that! However, I politely replied that the committee would be delighted.

There was a good turn-out, mostly out of curiosity, but we all felt a little sorry for the man who was going to lecture to *us* on agriculture. And when he appeared—a smartly dressed *gentleman*—we were really embarrassed. The poor fellow! However, we were polite. The chairman said we were glad to see him, etc.

Mr Esslemont then got to his feet. He asked if there was any special *aspect* of agriculture on which we preferred he would speak. Aspect? We didn't know agriculture had aspects. You just ploughed and sowed and harvested and fed the beasts. Did the poor man think we didn't know about that?

When we could not suggest any special aspect and he suggested a talk on grass and clover seed mixtures we felt very very sorry. Grass and clover seed mixtures! Just perennial rye grass, Italian, Red, White, and Alsyke clover that we had sown from time immemorial and knew as we knew the back of our hand. But again we were polite.

And lo! Mr Esslemont opened a black tin box. From thence he produced neatly assorted specimens of some forty different grasses, each bearing on a tag its botanical name and the name it was commonly known by. We had never heard of more than four of them.

Then he proceeded to explain that it was the "natural habit" of certain grasses to be "shallow feeders" while others were medium and still others deep-rooted feeders, others again only survived for one or two years while some lived on indefinitely—so that, if you wanted a really good crop of hay and a superior sole of pasture you had better sow a well-selected mixture. It was the first time in my life that I felt an utter ignoramus. Many a time in after years when giving much the same lecture did I wonder if ever I made anyone in my audience feel such an awful ass as Mr Esslemont made me feel that night.

CHAPTER VII

Rural Occupations—Troots at Midnight—Sunrise from the
Summit

THAT lecture on grass and clover seeds was followed by
several others on various agricultural "aspects" (to the
existence of which I was now thoroughly alive); relative
values of different varieties of cereals, potatoes, turnips,
and other crops; the scientific manuring of these in
accordance with their varying chemical needs and the
nature of the soil in which they grew; the "balancing"
of rations to the different classes of stock so as to get
maximum results with minimum waste—all such lectures
were to me as a key which opened the door to a fascinating
world of experiment and inquiry. The leaden heart
became light and joyous. Ordinary humdrum jobs were
humdrum no longer. Even a very elementary degree
of understanding of the scientific facts and processes which
underlay the most prosaic of field or midden operations
invested them with an absorbing interest.

In the next half-dozen years I carried out for Mr
Esslemont innumerable experiments for the purpose of
demonstrating to myself and my neighbours how we
might make better use of our time and land—and I am
fairly certain that never were such experiments more
meticulously carried out.

If only I could scrape together capital enough to take
a small farm of my own! With this as an incentive I took
on all sorts of piece-work or contract jobs, *e.g.*:

Felling Trees.—At five shillings per hundred, for larch-
trees averaging fifteen inches diameter. This was the
hardest and worst-paid job I ever tackled. We had to

walk three miles to the wood each morning and three miles home at night. It was in the short days of winter. We did the walking both ways in the dark. Every minute of daylight—bar half an hour for the flask of tea and the "piece"—it was dobb, saw, crash! dobb, saw, crash! until we reached the daily quota of 120 trees—which gave us three shillings per man per day. Last year it took me over two hours to fell one such tree and I didn't get over the effort for a week!

Fencing.—For the erection of a wood-and-wire fence of six wires and posts seven feet apart our contract price was a penny-farthing per yard. Two of us could each earn four shillings per day when things went well.

Ploughing.—For horseless neighbours—at ten shillings per day for self and pair of horses. There would be a total of forty to fifty of such days each year.

Harvesting.—Rate ten shillings per acre for cutting, lifting, binding, and stooking. With the scythe I would have an acre cut in about eight hours. Meanwhile, my helpmate, Old Kate (and she was a top-notcher at the job), had followed up with the lifting and binding. Together, in the next two hours we would complete the binding and stooking of the acre. I, as "contractor," kept six shillings to myself. Kate got four shillings— big money in those days, but believe me, we worked for it. If you want to be quite sure—try it!

Thinning Turnips.— Sixteen shillings per acre. In dirty stiff land and wet weather this was heart-breaking work, and could easily take six days to complete. Under best conditions I could rattle off an acre in four days. But a "careless" hoe can ruin a crop, and a high-quality standard of work was a *sine qua non* of the contract.

Clipping Turnips.—Six shillings and sixpence per acre for yellows and eight shillings for swedes. I knew a crack hand who could turn off his acre per day of either. Personally, I never quite got up to that standard. As a back-breaker, clipping swedes must stand alone; and on a winter's morning when the frosted leaves crackled in your hand it was most exquisite torture—for the first few minutes; then your fingers burned as with fire.

Making Bridle-paths, Grouse Butts, and Hill Drains.—For such contracts I was indebted to my spendthrift friends the *sasunnach* shooting tenants. For several weeks in summer three or four of us would take to the hills, returning only at week-ends for "tommy" (food supplies). One summer four of us lived for six weeks in a sort of cave near a burn. That was a terribly hot summer. It was impossible to work in the heat of the day, so we breakfasted at four-thirty, worked from five till ten A.M., rested on our heather bed in the cave till four P.M. and then worked till nine. Between nine and midnight (midges permitting) we fished for trout in the burn and set snares for hares, to augment our provender. One evening, in three hours, four of us caught a total of 365 trout—mostly small, but all of eatable size. As it happened, too, they were all required, as you will see.

At this particular time we were billeted in a corrugated-iron shed, known as "The Stables," near the base of the last steep climb to Ben Wyvis and miles from the nearest human habitation. On the night of the big catch it came on thick mist just as we turned in at midnight. Four of us slept in the one bed, which was a sort of wooden platform six feet square. At one A.M. we were wakened by the deuce of a row outside. A party from Dingwall were on their annual pilgrimage to view the sunrise from the summit of the ben. They had got completely wandered in the mist and now came bang up against our iron-clad home, on which they rattled their sticks with momentarily terrifying effect. Soon, though, we discerned human voices and gathered who they were. It was evident, too, that they had not neglected the liquid refreshment side of the holiday. One of the revellers recognised the place as "The Stables." They decided to enter and light a fire. Not one of the party had the remotest idea that the place was occupied. Just as they were about to enter, our batman, "Jock," quick to offer hospitality, appeared in natal state at the door, holding a lighted candle above his head. That crowd got the fright of their life: with a yell of terror they took to their heels and vanished in the mist. It took much shouted explanation and assurance of our mortal state before they were induced to return. There were over twenty all told. The stove with its leaky lum was set agoing. Jock presided at the frying-pan. In an hour all the trout, our week's roll of bacon, a few dozen eggs, and a considerable quantity of "Dalmore" disappeared in a sort of Dagdal orgy amongst the pilgrims. A number of them rested in "The Stables" while the remainder, under our guidance, set off for the top. Above the Fuaran Mòr we walked out of the mist into a crystal-clear atmosphere vibrant with the dawn of day. We reached the summit just in time to see the white light in the north-east change in turn to pale green, violet, copper, crimson, and finally the sun, lighting up the summits of a hundred hills, appeared a ball of burnished gold. Even the revellers were hushed to silent adoration. No wonder our ancestors worshipped the sun.

We in this country are surely a prize pack of grousers in regard to the climatic conditions under which we live on the earth's surface. We are always complaining—of what? Of climatic variations that people in most parts of the world would give much to possess. For surely nowhere else in all the world is there greater variety and beauty in this respect than in this wonderful little country of ours, with its shades of summer green, with its lochs and hills and heather; with those glorious evening twilights and the rosy spreading dawns. Ay, and there is a beauty, too, in the fertilising rains and in the frost and snow of winter, if we would but only see. . . .

CHAPTER VIII

A Domestic Bomb—Off on a New Tack—Reflections on the
Highland "Problem"

THIS chapter is going to have more of "I" in it even than
the others, but that can't be helped, as it is necessary to
tell how the Journey, at this stage, took a bend in a new
direction.

At the age of twenty-six I was what might fairly be
termed a practical crofter, skilled in a variety of country
crafts. My chief ambition in life was to save enough
money to enable me to secure the tenancy of a small farm.
Six months later I was a matriculated student of agriculture at Marischal College, Aberdeen, and destined for
a very different sort of career. This is how it happened.

One day in July, on returning home from some outside
job, I found Mr Esslemont waiting to see me. We walked
along the road together. He informed me that he had
been asked by the Governors of the Aberdeen and North
of Scotland College of Agriculture to look out for an
intelligent youth with a practical knowledge of crofting
and Gaelic who would take a course of training at Aberdeen with a view to appointment to the extension staff
of the College as Agricultural County Organiser in the
Hebrides. He had had his eye on me for some time and
was now asking if I could see my way clear to accept such
an offer. I would get financial assistance to the extent
of fifty pounds per annum while in training, and on taking
up the appointment would be put on a salary of eighty
pounds per annum with reasonable travelling expenses.

Only one with a previous experience similar to mine can
quite appreciate the stir which such a proposition caused
in my mind. A course at a College! A certain yearly

salary of eighty pounds! Travelling all over the
Hebrides! The whole thing was fantastic. Go? There
was no shadow of doubt that I would *like* to go; the
sobering question was: *could* I go?

My father—who had never quite recovered his health
and strength—had plenty to do in attending to the
innumerable lighter jobs on the place. For years I had
done all the heavy work, and had become an integral
part of the domestic team which kept the home together.
Mr Esslemont appreciated the difficulty. He did not
press for an immediate decision: it would do if I let him
know within a week or two. Meantime—not a word to
my parents or anybody else!

There was no sleep that night. Till six in the morning
I thought and planned, seeking for a way that would let
me go, yet leave the home intact. A hired man, to do
the ploughing and heavy work, must be found. After
much cogitation I decided who the man should be—if
he could be got to come. Let me say here, he did come,
and proved so thoroughly unsatisfactory that he had to
go within a month; and during the next four years some
half a dozen men came and went in embarrassing
succession. I suspect the meticulous standard of work
demanded by my father—which he had got from me as
a result of early training and unquestioned insistence—
had a good deal to do with these frequent changes.
Anyhow, luckily, I did not foresee them!

Finance had to be carefully worked out. The fifty
pounds annual grant would do little more than pay for
the ploughman. There was no family fund to draw on.
That meant I would require to keep myself during the
training period in Aberdeen. I had saved thirty pounds
in cash and owned—as my own property, grazing on a
neighbouring croft which I had rented—six stirks and
twenty sheep. With luck these would realise some

seventy pounds—giving a total of, say, a hundred pounds to cover living in a city for two years. In my ignorance of city life, and all that that almost inevitably involved in the way of spending, a hundred pounds seemed fairly ample. Here—to anticipate again—I was soon to realise my mistake, and some heroic wind-raising measures had to be resorted to before the two years were out.

But the biggest hurdle of all was that I would require to break the news to my father. For in those days, in our circles, despite extraordinarily strong (but inarticulate) ties of family affection there was a stern lack of chumminess between sons and fathers, which made the thought of having to tackle my male parent in the matter almost paralysing. I felt like one about to throw a bomb in the family kitchen!

But, anyhow, it had to be done; for my mind was made up, and that very day I placed the whole proposition before him. He listened without a word while I unfolded the story of the opportunity which had come my way and my plans thereanent. When I finished with:

"But, of course, if you think it can't be done—well, I'll just stay on," to my surprise and unspeakable joy he just said:

"Well, boy, I will not advise you in a matter of that kind: you must make your own decision. All I can say is that, if you see your way clear yourself, I will not stand in the way, and if you go I hope you will make a success of it—and we will manage at home *some* way." Somehow that made me feel that I had never quite understood my father before. I now felt such a surge of pride in him and such gratitude towards him that I fear I fell from the old tradition by indulging in a momentary mumbled confession of such emotions—which greatly embarrassed us both.

That was in July. By the end of September the crop

was all in and thatched; everything about the place in apple-pie order; the new ploughman engaged; the stirks and sheep converted into cash; my trunk packed and everything ready for my journey to the opening of the session at Marischal College, Aberdeen, on the 8th of October.

Now, after over thirty years of the comparatively sheltered, genteel, non-perspiring career, first of an Agricultural Lecturer, and later of a Civil Servant, I much doubt whether the change-over has been to my advantage in the things that really matter in life; but I am certain that no such argument would have weighed with me when the opportunity for change came. Then I just grasped it with both hands—and I have no regrets. I would only add this reflection:

Every now and again a new champion enters the public arena and demands the re-peopling of the Highland straths and glens. The thesis that it is a good thing for the country to have the biggest possible number of people living contentedly in the Highlands needs no elaboration. Unfortunately, its practical application is beset with difficulties. For some men and women of philosophic outlook life on the land—cultivating, seeding, tending and harvesting of crops, the breeding and nurturing of stock—even if unaccompanied by much in the way of monetary profit, is of absorbing interest. They are happy.

But such are in a minority. The majority of agriculturists, big and little, are ordinary, mercenary human beings, maybe enjoying some of the æsthetic pleasures of the life, but grimly materialistic in desiring monetary reward; and when this does not come they are dissatisfied and, as opportunity offers, go elsewhere. This has happened in the case of a great many crofters and their families throughout the Highlands in the past half-century: and were it not for that sense of filial duty which is so strong in crofting families the exodus would have been much greater. These are the simple facts—facts which "reformers" seem to be ignorant of, or forget. The truth is that those Utopian dreams of regenerating the Highlands are indulged in mainly by prosperous, elderly, estimable people who forsook the Highlands in their teens for "success" elsewhere and now cherish sentimental recollections of their early years. Life in a Highland glen seems to them a grand thing—in retrospect; and (now that they have grown older) maybe in prospect. But it didn't appeal to them when they were young any more than it appeals to young people of to-day.

It is unreasonable to expect educated young people to stay contented and happy in an unremunerative calling while bigger prizes are offered elsewhere; not even for their country's good or in order that a few reformers and politicians may reap public honour or continue to sit in the high places.

In this connection it is an interesting fact that, as a result of prolonged unemployment in industrial centres prior to the War, and now of the precarious thing which the War has proved life in a big city to be, a new light is coming to many: new standards of values are being set up. It is now a matter of general comment among young people in both town and country that a job in a city is a very uncertain thing. Conversely, many of them have come to appreciate the solid advantages that go with life on the land. To a young countryman a job at three or four pounds per week looked wealth. Now, in the city, he knows that even when such a wage is assured it has a habit of vanishing in umpteen ways of which a countryman wots not, and he realises he would be much better off in the country, earning a quarter of that amount in addition to the potatoes and milk and butter and cream and poultry and eggs and the dozen other substantial things which he could produce on his own holding. He also knows that in the city he is more or less of a serf, while on his holding he is a king in his castle.

By all sensible means let us seek to re-people the Highlands and so strengthen the strands of the fabric of nation; and if I were asked to state in two words the improvements which would do more than any other to make life on the land in the Highlands more attractive these words would be *roads* and *houses*. Not merely main roads, but roads —and good roads—to and through every glen and clachan and croft, and my houses would be of attractive design, with hot and cold water and electric light and power. Most of the many other necessary improvements would follow: but it is futile for those elderly sentimentalists or pushing politicians to imagine they can realise their dream by talking down to and advising the young folk to stay in, or return to, the Highlands. Young people nowadays resent being talked down to, and are perfectly capable of deciding a matter of this kind for themselves.

PART II

CHAPTER IX

The Novice at work—Contrary Winds—Keeping the Horns on!—
Elphin and Cnocan—Mistaken for a Tramp—Tinker Hospitality
—The Fight at the Inn—Conscientious Objectors

As a pioneer instructor in the science and art of agriculture
I had a wide territory, comprising as it did not only the
whole of the Outer Hebrides—"From Butt of Lewis to
Barra Head"—but also the western seaboard from
Durness to Glenelg. A faithful "Rudge" was my main
means of locomotion. On it I did around four thousand
miles per annum. Soon its beautiful nickel-plate and
polished ebony succumbed to the island elements, to be
succeeded by a uniform rusty hue, to which one became
reconciled in the knowledge that it couldn't go worse and
conferred complete immunity in the matter of future
cleaning; but in the qualities that mattered that bicycle
was superb. With unfailing efficiency it carried my then
180-pound person (plus rucksack, spraying machine, and
other paraphernalia that sometimes weighed over half
a hundredweight) upwards of 20,000 miles of the worst
roads in Britain, often battered with rain, caked with mud
or soused in sea-water—and it was still going strong
twenty years after it had passed from my ownership.

For the first winter I (full of enthusiasm and in-
experience) prepared a neatly tabulated itinerary designed
to avoid loss of a single day or hour. Och, och!

On the Monday morning that was to be the first day of
a succession of visits and meetings during a week in South
Uist I was not a little annoyed to see rain falling somewhat

heavily. The night before had been fine and promising, so that this bolt from the blue was all the more so.

"It can only be a shower?" I surmised to the landlady, whose "Och, maybe, and maybe no," sounded rather ominous.

Reluctantly I postponed the start for an hour; but the "maybe no" was right. Before the end of the hour a gale (as I then deemed it) was driving a mixture of rain and hail and sleet and snow with remorseless fury across that rather unbieldy country. That continued all day, so I sent off half a dozen telegrams cancelling meetings and wrote a long letter to friends on the mainland telling of the terrible storm—two things which, in light of further experience, have often caused me to smile!

On Tuesday the storm was worse; on Wednesday it was still crescendo, and so it continued for the week. By this time it was being borne in on me that storm-severity conceptions are largely a matter of upbringing: that the people of the island were going about their ordinary avocations—with oilskins and sou'westers their only evidence of respect for the elements. So on the following Monday I pushed off on my Rudge, determined to have *some* entry for the official diary. There was still more than a capful of wind and occasional showers. That day, too, I observed for the first time a peculiar phenomenon in regard to the winds of the Hebrides: *no matter what direction you may be cycling in, the wind is always against you*. Meteorologists may dispute that statement, but I will never concede more than that it may be a slight exaggeration. This day the wind was dead against me to Dalibrough.

"I'll get a side-birl from there to Pollachar," thinks I. But from Dalibrough to Pollachar it was head-on again! At every little rise in the road I had to get off and push. On one such occasion I noticed a small tent by the roadside, heavily staked down with ropes, and with smoke fitfully issuing from its narrow doorway. Near the tent were a lot of Highland cows, and I noticed that one of these had a horseshoe dangling over her nose and suspended by a rope tied round the horns. Parking the bicycle in the roadside ditch I made for the tent, in hope of shelter from an oncoming shower.· A voice in choicest brogue invited me "insoide," and in minutes I was enjoying the beautifullest "cup-o-tay" from the jovial Pat who, it transpired, was also new to this "counthrie." The horseshoe on the cow's nose had intrigued me, and before starting off again in a glint of watery sunshine I asked Pat if he had any idea of its purpose or meaning. Was it some local superstition, or what?

"Shure I didn't noatice it before at all at all!" said Pat. Then with a stab of Irish humour: "But, bejabbers, it'll be to kape the horns from blowing aff wid the wind, for the loikes of this counthrie for wind I nivir saw in me bliddy loife!"

As a matter of interest I may explain that later I saw many cows similarly adorned, and learned that the horseshoe is put there for the purpose of restraining a beast with a bad reputation for fighting and bullying others in the fold. The plan is said to be very effective too.

There was that other day of cycling—years later—with its one adventure after another.

If you look at a map of the Highlands you will see in the gusset of Sutherland that stabs into Ross-shire the names "Elphin" and "Cnocan." In the common phrase of the unthinking these Highland hamlets are "miles from anywhere"—implying a superior status for the "anywheres" and a corresponding insignificance for the places so far from them. In reality, of course, it is the other way about. For, in the things that really matter, it is the Elphins and the Cnocans of the world that are to be congratulated and envied, and the "anywheres" that are to be commiserated: the poor cities with their glare and their blare and their shams and their shames.

Anyhow, notwithstanding my views of such things, and my knowledge of the standard of social amenities and natural dignity that is so characteristic of quiet country places, Elphin and Cnocan came as a delightful surprise. In most places I had first visited in my official capacity, just what I was and represented seemed somewhat hazy in the local mind. Not so in Elphin: there they knew all about the Agricultural College and its activities. They knew of my appointment; they even wondered why I hadn't paid them a visit sooner! So I didn't have to explain myself. That *was* a new and pleasant experience.

At the meeting that night in the joint recreation hall and reading-room—well supplied, by the way, with daily and weekly newspapers and a selection of the best monthly magazines—there was not a vestige of the awkwardness which had been a characteristic of many of my first meetings. Without any palaver one man moved that Mr So-and-so take the chair. Mr So-and-so, in response to general acclamation, did so. He thanked them for the honour and made just the correct introductory remarks with the ease and practice of a Member of Parliament.

On inquiry later I was given to understand that the quite remarkable up-to-dateness of these townships originated years earlier with a schoolmaster of progressive views. In face of considerable old-world opposition he conducted *secular* as well as sacred singing classes, founded a literary and debating society, collected funds for the erection of a hall where the members could meet and read and debate in the long winter evenings—yes, and dance too!—thereby winning for himself the anathemas of the old and the enthusiastic regard of the young, and finally of the whole community—— But I started to tell of the adventure that befell on a day of cycling.

It was in Elphin one Friday afternoon that I got a telegram to say my brother had arrived home on holiday from South Africa. I had planned to cycle home on the Saturday in any case, and now decided to start off straight away. The distance was fifty-seven miles. It was now four o'clock. I should make it by ten or so.

Passing Ullapool I decided to carry on rather than waste time over a meal. Bitterly did I regret this an hour later when walking up the Coire Shalach brae. There hunger assailed me, and a cloud of weariness. In desperation I determined to call at a keeper's house for something to eat. My knock brought, not the keeper's wife, but a stranger, to the door. But "hunger's power is strong"; so I doffed the battered hat and made known my need. Very likely I did look the perfect tramp. Anyhow, the woman (wife of an English butler, I learned later) was taking no chances. She practically ordered me off the premises!

Indignation overcame hunger as I strode away; but that lasted only for a little while. Soon the awful urge to eat came on with renewed force. A mile past the keeper's I saw, some two hundred yards off the road, a tinker's encampment, with its three rugged horses, two dogs, a few hens, and a swarm of children all complete. There were still three miles to walk and then six to cycle before I could reach Altguish inn.

I went straight to the tinker's tent. The "Royal Family" had but newly arrived. A swarthy woman in the thirties was preparing a meal at the camp-fire.

"Good evening," I greeted her. "I have come a long way and there's still a long road in front. I'm very hungry. Could you give me a cup of tea or anything to eat?"

"Surely!" came the hearty response.

"I thought I might get something from the keeper's wife," I added, "but she is not staying in the house just now."

"Don't I know that! Didn't I call there an hour ago and found only yon blank, blank, blankety blank of a creature who said she would send for the police!" my new hostess indignantly informed me.

In minutes she had spread on the grass a white cloth, with bread and butter and honey and two boiled eggs; there was a large bowl of fragrant tea to wash it down. That meal still remains in my mind a rare and refreshing feast.

I was terribly grateful and said so, but a far-off hint of financial recompense was emphatically turned down.

"Not a penny," said she; "I never know when I may be needing a cup of tea myself."

In excellent trim, though now well behind scheduled time, I sped on my way. It was after ten o'clock when I approached the old inn at Altguish—still eighteen miles from home—but the night was fine, and it would never do to pass genial old Davie of the inn without a word in the by-going.

"It's the good Lord that sent you," said Davie in the Gaelic, "and you must stay the night."

But no: I must push on—just a shout on the way, etc.

"Oh! but you must stay," Davie insisted. "There are two scoundrels of tramps in the kitchen. They were drunk when they arrived at midday; they had a bottle with them. They are now very drunk, and threatening to burn the house down if they don't get more whisky."

Just then we heard loud voices in the kitchen.

"There they go again," said Davie (who was old and very lame). "For God's sake go and try to get them to go away."

I had a keek in at the kitchen door. The tramps were displaying the contents of a tin box—some bootlaces, a few collar-studs, a box of hairpins, and such like treasure —and offering the whole job lot for a half-mutchkin of whisky. The women looked scared but refused to trade. The tramps were very tight, but determined; they threatened unspeakable consequences if whisky wasn't immediately forthcoming.

One was a sturdily built man, wearing a short beard and a semi-nautical suit. The other was a weedy-looking specimen of pallid countenance. The inn was miles from the nearest house. They had never dreamed of anyone being about the place but the two old women and the lame Davie. It must have come as a shock to them, therefore, to hear a strange voice say: "Hello! Hello, gentlemen! And what is all the row about?"

Paleface simply wilted and sneaked outside. Not so the sailor.

"And what the h—— is that to you?" he demanded, coming towards me in anything but chummy mood.

But before he was prepared for it I got a good grip of his jersey high up at the back, rushed him along the lobby, out at the front door, and landed him in the side-drain across the road. Davie promptly locked the front door, while I bolted round the house and in at the back door, which we also locked. So there we were: all trouble over and a peaceful night ahead. We thought the nightcap well earned.

Soon we were disillusioned: the sailor came round to opposite our window and yelled his frank opinion of us. It was far from flattering. But it was only when he started again his threat of setting fire to the house that we took serious notice. I tried to reassure Davie, but he was highly nervous. When he heard the scratching of matches he got really scared.

"There's a cartload of bog-fir outside the back door," he remembered, "and it will burn like paraffin!"

Meantime the sailor, at the back door, was demanding admittance, and in spite of my remonstrance Davie went to open it.

"Wait," I insisted, "and I'll go out and speak to him, but he must not come in."

I opened the door just enough to allow me to slip out. There was the sailor, with an ugly-looking knobkerry of fir-root in his hand.

"If you don't let me in I'll bash your bloody brains out," said he, frothing mad. There was no doubt he meant it too. Now, I was never much "a man of my hands." Indeed, I have always preferred sweet reason-ableness to fisticuffs in an argument. But clearly the smooth answer would not serve here. So with my fist I hit him on the chin as hard as I could. It must have been pretty hard for, to my astonishment, he dropped like an old log. For a few moments I had a wild fear that I had killed him! But like a Jack-in-the-box he was up and kicked me one in the stomach, that partially winded me and nearly made me vomit. Then I went mad. There followed the wildest rough-and-tumble of my life. It was an all-out catch-as-catch-can and no-quarter affair. We rolled over and over, first one on top, then the other; crashed through the garden paling, flattened Davie's cabbages and brussels sprouts, and got badly lacerated amongst the gooseberry bushes. Davie was hopping about on his crutch hoping to get in a helpful blow with his heavy iron-clad stick.

"Will I hit him?" yelled Davie.

"Yes!" I bawled, not in the least concerned with the niceties; and Davie brought a terrific whack down *on my thigh*!

I howled—and cursed—and very nearly fainted with

the pain. Only dire necessity kept me conscious and enabled me to continue the fight.

I am morally certain that if that sailor hadn't been drinking all day he could—and would—have murdered me. He was as strong as a horse, and had some scientific holds that I knew nothing of. But his wind was going: he couldn't stand the pace. I managed to wriggle on top and all of a sudden the fight went out of him. Davie brought a plough-rein, with which we trussed him up good and tight. We left him thus, lying amongst the ruined vegetables, while we went to remove the blood and grime of battle and apply sticking-plaster to the bigger wounds. There was also a matter of refreshment attended to.

In half an hour the sailor was howling for mercy. The rein was cutting into his arms and legs.

"For God's sake cut this bloody rope!" he pleaded.

Perhaps I did a very foolish thing, but who could see and hear a man suffering like that? Anyhow, I undid the rope. The "word of honour" which I had extracted from him as a preliminary very nearly didn't stand the strain when he found himself freed again; but the sight of Davie's iron-clad stick—which I now controlled— saved it. He walked stiffly but in the right direction.

Next morning at six Davie came to my room in great agitation. Our two friends of the night before were sound asleep in the stable! When they wakened up the whole trouble would begin again! I would be gone and not a soul would come near the place till the mail coach came at noon!

It was arranged that the sleepers would be left undisturbed. In passing Garve I would call at the police station and ask the constable to start for Altguish immediately.

The constable was doing his morning ablutions in a tin

basin of cold water at the gable-end of his house when I arrived at eight o'clock. He was off on his bicycle within twenty minutes.

I got home in time for a late breakfast. In the afternoon I changed into another suit and started for Achterneed station to join the train for Dingwall. That day the train was unusually punctual. I nearly missed it. It was actually moving off when at the end of a two minutes' desperate sprint I just managed to tumble in. Panting, I sat down. Then I looked at the others in the compartment. Paleface and Sailor!—handcuffed together with the policeman in charge! I nearly jumped out again. But, taking my cue from the Arm-of-the-Law (who betrayed not a glint of recognition), I soon saw that neither prisoner was likely to link up this well-dressed young man with the ruffian of last night at Altguish; nor did they.

Next week the Chief Constable of Ross-shire thanked me for "aiding the police," and (unofficially) complimented me on the battered condition of the sailor's features.

And now for a confession—and a bone for the psychologists to chew on. That was my only fight as a grown-up man and I *enjoyed it.* In fact, it gave me the grandest thrill of my life. Which makes me to believe that:

(1) In primitive man there is a natural lust for blood and battle.

(2) All our "civilisation" hasn't succeeded in greatly altering man's primordial instincts.

(3) In certain circumstances the most conscientious of conscientious objectors would fight like a fiend—and enjoy it too.

CHAPTER X

Restrained Enthusiasm—Calum—Commercials' Tall Tales

WHEN I went first to the islands I was full of enthusiasm for my work, but ignorant of most of the agricultural customs and practices of the district. Many of the latter struck me as old-fashioned and in direct opposition to the accepted principles and practices of good husbandry in other districts. A little reflection and observation, however, soon caused me to modify my view and to realise that there was some sound basis of common sense and experience for many of the accepted ways of doing things out there. Consequently, any visions I might have had of rapidly revolutionising the agriculture of the islands soon vanished.

"Go dead slow"; "Don't pose as a wise man from the East"; "Look for ways in which you *can* really suggest improvement" were some of the warnings I gave myself. And even then I would require to go very canny because, when a man is accustomed to do certain work in a certain way—and his father and grandfather did it that way too —he very naturally resents any tactless suggestions for "improvement" from an outsider—and a comparative youngster at that. It was with a full appreciation of these facts and with appropriate humility that I one day decided to approach Calum on the question of the best method of sowing corn.

Now the native method of sowing the corn had for some time been in my mind as a possible subject for demonstrating a more up-to-date method. It *had* struck me as rather contradictory that when sowing corn a man should step backwards instead of forward. Actually that was what I found. The sower started at the end of the ploughed rig and, stepping *backwards*, scattered by one hand the seed from a pail which he carried in the other. The sowing was done by irregular, spasmodic jerks of the hand and the sower stepped backwards to do a new area when he had sown the part in front right up to his feet. The general effect was that of a man shaking pepper over a gigantic plate of soup. The process was terribly slow; it would take the best part of a day to sow a couple of acres. While the sower (usually the father) was busy in the soup-peppering manner the son, with the horses yoked in the harrows, rested till the rig was sown. He then got busy with the harrows while the sower rested on the seed-bag and had a smoke. By the time the sower had had his rest and smoke the horses and their attendant were ready to rest again till the next rig was sown—and so on, turn about till the job was finished. It was all very interesting and picturesque but far from speedy—and in that uncertain climate often resulted in protracted sowing, with correspondingly late harvest.

Calum had just started sowing a three-acre field on the morning that I decided to make my venture. His son and horses were there to harrow when they got the opportunity and the work was proceeding in the good old-fashioned way. Calum and myself exchanged the usual courtesies relating to weather prospects, family welfare, etc. We spoke in Gaelic and the whole of our subsequent conversation was in that language, and this tale loses a lot in the English telling. I then remarked that he was busy at the sowing.

"Very busy," said Calum.

"You will take a good while to sow the field," I opinioned.

"Yes, indeed," agreed Calum. "It will take me all of to-day and maybe a bit of to-morrow too."

"You have never tried any other way of sowing?" ventured myself.

"Other way?" inquired Calum. "No. I never heard of any other way; and am I not busy enough?"

"Oh, yes indeed," I agreed, "you are busy enough, and making a very good job, too; but where I come from we sow in a different way. It will not be any better than your own way, but I do believe it might be quicker."

"Indeed?" said Calum, a little curious.

"Yes indeed, I think so," said I.

"Indeed," said Calum again; "and what way would you be sowing it?"

"Och!" I protested, "it will not be any better than your own way, but it will be quicker right enough"; and then I added: "If you do not mind I will sow a bit to let you see."

"Surely," invited Calum, "indeed I would like fine to see you doing it."

The pail was just an ordinary pail, but I had to make the best of it. I tied a piece of rope by the middle, close to where the handle joined the pail at the side furthest from my tummy; then passed the ends of the rope round my waist, tying them firmly at my back. This made a sort of improvised seed-container. I then suggested to Calum that his wife and daughter should come to the field with other pails to keep me supplied with seed; but as a pail of seed was sufficient to keep Calum sowing for quite a while he couldn't see any necessity for this; he himself would replenish my "box" when required. So my first pail was filled by Calum, and as I crossed over to my starting-place at the end of the rig Calum sat down on the seed-bag and proceeded to fill his pipe preparatory to watching the performance.

Here I may say without boasting that I was (and I am still) a really good two-handed sower. On this occasion

I stepped out at my very best, broadcasting the seed in those rhythmical rainbow sweeps that always give the sower a peculiar joy. After advancing thirty yards or so I stopped to get Calum's opinion of the job. Calum was astounded. He hadn't even completed the filling of the pipe. The sight of his seed being scattered in this quick and seeming reckless fashion was too much for him.

"What do you think of it?" I inquired.

"May the Lord look upon me!" replied Calum, "but I'm not sure. It looks a very careless way of throwing the seed about, anyway. But wait till I see."

He came over and carefully examined the bit I had sown, and to my relief pronounced: "It *looks* right enough, whatever."

On this I assured him I had sown fields and fields of corn in that way and that the crops had grown quite well. I offered to carry on and finish the field for him.

"Carry on," agreed Calum, "and I will get the wife and lassie out to keep you supplied with seed."

When the wife and daughter came out Calum's field became the scene of unwonted activity. For effect I deliberately sowed faster than ever I had done before. The two women had to run to keep me going. The horses were nearly running in the harrows but couldn't catch up.

I had taken the precaution of ascertaining from Calum the exact quantity of seed he customarily sowed in that field. He told me in *pecks*, so that I had to do some mental gymnastics to translate pecks to bushels. I took good care to come out just right at the finish. In less than an hour the job was completed, but by this time there was a gallery of a dozen neighbours who had walked over to ascertain the cause of all the commotion on Calum's field. They carefully examined the still unharrowed part and were frankly outspoken with their comments. In the

interest of fair play one man was constrained to admit it
"*looked* right enough anyway," but this qualified optimism
was douched by another who dolefully remarked:

"Och, yes; it may *look* right enough; *but the man who
lives longest will see what will come of work of this kind!*"

Calum himself was a complete convert. He said he
was in his eighty-fourth year but, old as he was, he would
like to have a try of the new way. (Actually he didn't,
but I did have the satisfaction later of initiating his son
to the sowing "step and cast," with sand from the shore
as "seed" and in a "box" made by the local blacksmith.)
Meantime Calum proceeded to remark on the extraordinary wonders a man might see in the course of a long
life.

"Of course," he remarked, "I might hear of the like
of this, but *seeing is believing*. Look you," he explained,
"some of us have never been to the mainland of Scotland.
For myself I have never been further than the Pier in my
life, but we are not so simple as to believe everything we
are told! And indeed some of the commercial travellers
that come to the shop, though very nice men, are not
above telling us some tall stories."

I agreed that some of the commercials' tales might
require a pinch of salt.

"Indeed yes," concurred Calum. "There was one of
them here a fortnight ago—a very nice man too—but
och! the lies he tried to make me believe in half an
hour!"

"Ay, ay," said I.

"Yes indeed," said Calum, shaking his white beard;
"and do you know what he was trying to make me
believe at last?"

"No," said I.

"Yes," said Calum, digging the joke into my ribs and
chuckling at the recollection of this Ananias of the road,

"*that they can hatch out the chickens nowadays without hens at all!*"

We all laughed heartily at the audacity of the man who could so presume on native credulity.

It is interesting to know that within a very short time there were several incubators in use in the islands and that Calum lived long enough to revise his opinion of the commercial's veracity, for when I visited the island ten years later this delightful old man had not yet passed on to The Land of the Ever Young.

CHAPTER XI

ON the old croft we had a great big barn; at any rate, being the biggest "room" I had seen bar the church and the big classroom at the school, it seemed to me to be a tremendous size. I could hardly believe myself recently when, measuring out the barn from its old *larach* (site), I was forced to the conclusion it couldn't have been so terribly big after all.

Anyhow, anything is big or little only relatively, and I prefer to think of the old barn as very big.

And what tales that old barn could have told had its walls the power of speech! New Year dances, wedding dances, political meetings, Land League meetings, prayer-meetings, christenings—the old barn gave impartial hospitality to all.

For a real big occasion like a wedding dance care was taken to have the barn as clear of straw, etc., as possible. What little straw or sheaves there were, were piled up neatly at one end, and formed an excellent perch from the top of which we youngsters could look with some amazement at the unwonted riotous ongoings of our elders.

Who, for instance, that had only seen *Donncha Beag* plodding with heavy step in the wake of the harrows, or solemnly wending his way to or from church, would recognise in him yon sprightly lad who flung his feet so high at the *righil a' phosaidh* (wedding dance) that he would kick the candle off its stone wall-bracket six feet off the floor, and who, at the change-over from the reel to the reel o' Tulloch, would give a hooch that would all but lift the thatch from the rafters! *M'eudal air!*

And again, under the same wall-bracket, I have seen the same Little Duncan of the dance sit at prayer-meeting with devout and solemn countenance drinking in the terrors of hell and damnation with never a doubt of their reality!

One of the biggest wedding dances I can remember was when an uncle of mine got married. For that night, at any rate, the rather drab routine of the croft was forgotten in dance and song and revelry.

One of the brightest and gayest of the guests was a deer-stalker who had come for the occasion from his home in a glen fully twenty miles away.

I can see him yet, with red whiskers and redder cheeks and tall athletic figure, getting full value out of the general merriment—and what a shock it was when news came to the glen within a very short time that our robust, jovial stalker friend was dead—treacherously killed by one of his own stags!

The story, as I remember it, was that the stags were being hand-fed during a heavy snowstorm. In such circumstances, of course, stags become as tame as sheep. One day this stalker had been at either church or a funeral —I forget which—and on returning, without waiting to change into his ordinary tweeds, he went out with a feed of maize to the stags. A big stag—and known to be rather cheeky—either mistook him for a stranger or objected to the dark clothes and set on him furiously, with the tragic result that so awed us.

That was the first time I realised that stags could on occasion be very dangerous animals.

I had another sharp lesson in that direction many years later. A friendly keeper and myself were having a day at the hares in October. Late in the afternoon a wounded hare crossed through the deer fence into the forest and dropped dead within view, but some two hundred yards in. Leaving my gun at the fence I went through to retrieve the hare. There was some very rough bouldery ground immediately beyond, but I never noticed any deer there, and even if I had would probably have thought nothing of it. I picked up the hare, and was more than half-way back to the fence when I heard a noise behind me. I turned round to look for the cause of it, and there was a big stag coming straight at me at full gallop! In a flash I realised that I was in a very perilous position and one that brooked of no delay. Believe me, there was none! At the time I didn't think, I ran! The other side of that fence was the most desired thing in my world! How I did it I can't yet understand, but I did manage like a rabbit to shoot through between two wires of the fence with about five feet to spare between my pants and the antlers of the infuriated beast. It didn't take me long, now on the safe side of the fence, to grasp my loaded gun. My recent pursuer, evidently appreciating the altered circumstances, had about-turned and fled, but I did have the satisfaction of getting a fairly effective "right and left" of No. 4's well planted round his apology for a tail!

It was a lucky escape, and my only regret was that there was no official timekeeper with a stop-watch, for I am morally certain that on that occasion I made a time for the hundred yards that would stagger Jesse Owens!

You may well think that that experience should have been sufficient to last me a lifetime and that in future, unless adequately armed, I would give stags in October the widest of wide berths.

Yet there is some contrary streak in most of us, and it wasn't so very many years afterwards that I let myself in for another real scare with a stag.

One day in late October I was plugging along on my Rudge on the road from Lochmaddy to Locheport. The road for most of its length of eight miles passes through open moorland. About half-way along I heard a stag roaring on my left. I came off the bicycle to look. He stood on the skyline some six hundred yards away and was facing at right angles to my line of vision. A right noble silhouette he made too, as he roared another challenge to any stag that cared to take it up.

Little dreaming of consequences so embarrassing, I thought I would like to try to see how near I could achieve to a realistic "roar" myself. With the notes of the stag's last bellow still fresh in my ears I let out the best imitation "roar" I could. It must have been a surprising success, for like shot that stag whipped round to face my direction.

"Gosh!" I thought, "that's interesting."

He gave another roar and tossed some heather with his horns. Elated with success I gave yet another "roar." I had no sooner done it than I began to realise what an idiot I was. As swift and smooth as a swallow that stag came galloping towards me! While he was still some four hundred yards away I jumped on the bicycle and was off as hard as I could pedal it. But a glance over my left shoulder showed me that my utmost speed was less than half that of the stag.

Scarcely realising what I was doing I came off the bicycle with some wild and futile idea of throwing it over his antlers when he actually attacked me. To my unspeakable relief, as soon as I got off the bicycle and stood still I saw that the stag stopped too.

He was now about a hundred and fifty yards away. He roared a roar that made the hills echo and re-echo for miles round and gave me the queerest of colly-wobbly feelings in the pit of my stomach. I did *not* answer that challenge! The stag stood staring with eyes which, even at that distance, I could see flashing. He roared and he roared again. I thought of all sorts of plans for escape, well knowing they were equally futile. Two or three times I tried to slide away on the bicycle, but every time I did that the brute raced towards me again till I stopped. Then he stopped and roared. How long this cat-and-mouse business went on I couldn't say, but to me it seemed hours of acutest funk, with that maddened beast now not fifty yards off, and not a house within two miles.

And just when I sort of made up my mind to face the inevitable as bravely as I could, if that stag didn't about-turn and flee as if the devil were biting at his heels! I nearly collapsed with relief and had to pull myself together.

It was with a mightily thankful heart I saw the last of the stag as he spanged over the skyline.

Then I cycled on towards the road end, leading to the gamekeeper's cottage. There I met the keeper, to whom I told my story. I was not a little hurt to notice he was inclined to be incredulous, but after a bit he had to believe me.

"What sort of a beast was it?" he asked.

"It was a fairly big stag, blackish at the neck and a nine-pointer," I replied, rather annoyed.

"Oh! I know that beast, and indeed I'm not saying but he could be nasty enough," admitted the keeper. "What did you do that set him off like yon?" he inquired.

"Nothing that I know of: he just went off all of a sudden."

"When did you light that cigarette?" he asked.

Truth to tell, till he asked, I hadn't noticed I was smoking a cigarette at all. It was now nearly finished.

"Really, I can't tell you," was my reply.

"Well," said he, "I can tell you. You lit that cigarette

at the moment the stag ran away—and it was the flash of the match which probably saved your life. It is not the first time I have seen a stag bolt at the flash of a light."

Well, well! That was a tip I'm not likely to forget— but indeed it isn't me that will invite trouble like yon again!

CHAPTER XII

Ablutions on the House-tops—Cracking Cockles

In the Highlands the crow has ever been held in somewhat sinister repute. Always it has been credited with something more than mere bird-wisdom. Only a very reckless person would deliberately destroy a rookery, even if its proximity to the house made it an annual nuisance. There was no harm in shooting young crows at the rookery: that was an annual sport. But destroying the rookery itself was a very different matter—a very unlucky thing to do.

Who that was brought up in the country has not observed the cunning of the crow on potato-stealing bent? While the crows are intent on digging out the potatoes, one at least of their number mounts guard on a fence-post or tree near by, so that never a chance of a shot at the raiders can a man get.

Their sense of location of the potato in the earth, too, is rather uncanny. With seldom-erring accuracy the bill is bored into the side of the drill right to the tuber at its middle. Another well-directed stab and the potato is impaled by the bill. Off flies Mr Crow to some spot where he can guzzle in safety on his titbit—leaving a hitherto flourishing potato-plant to wilt and die and a farmer to grouse at yet another of his innumerable afflictions.

Often I have seen a kestrel—which had probably been showing too keen an interest in the crow's nursery—harried to distraction by a crowd of crows. Sometimes too I have seen the crows' attack strengthened by a few gulls, and even by some linnets, who joined forces to teach a lesson to the common enemy.

I did not know that crows ate mice until one day a good many years ago. It must have been about the month of June, for we were threshing the last stack in the yard. As is not uncommon in the case of last stacks, this one harboured swarms of mice. These we ruthlessly slew with the joint help of dogs, cats, and sticks.

Out of curiosity a few of us youngsters counted the dead mice and placed them in a *dalachan*—a sort of corn riddle, or container, made by stretching a calf-skin over an ordinary riddle-frame. There were over 300 mice, and the *dalachan* was placed on the top of a strainer post before we went in to dinner.

During the meal we heard an awful rumpus, and on looking out we saw a great number of crows struggling and fighting with each other to get at the mice. Off went every lucky crow with a mouse in his beak. In less than five minutes not a mouse was left in the *dalachan*!

Quite recently, in Thurso, the hotel in which I usually stay was packed to the door with summer visitors. I counted myself lucky in getting an attic room very high up. It was a delightful room though, and gave one a sort of thrill, as of sleeping near the top of a lighthouse.

Bright and early in the morning I was awake and enjoying the luxury of lying in a comfortable bed and looking out of the open window at the bonnie sky which you sometimes get in the far north. By shifting my head slightly I found my view somewhat obstructed by a chimney-stalk whose top was little more than level with my window. There were four cans on top of that chimney. From the volume of smoke which issued from one can it was obvious that down below preparations for feeding the multitude were already under way. The other three cans —probably bedroom vents—were "idle." The smoking can was second from the left and the smoke from it blew over the two cans on the right.

While I was speculating on the inequalities of this life's luck, which permitted of my lying snugly in bed the while a fellow-creature was already afoot and labouring for my further comfort in the shape of an appetising breakfast, what should hop on to the idle can on the extreme left but a crow. He wasn't more than twenty feet from my bed. He alighted on the side of the can furthest from the smoking can. Then he side-stepped round till he was on the side nearest the smoke. To my amusement he stretched his head over into the smoke, but withdrew it in a moment and vigorously shook it, as if the smoke were irritating his eyes. But again and again he did it, and then—after obviously and comically making up his mind to take the plunge—he hopped on to the far rim of the smoking can, spread first one wing and then another right into the thickest of the smoke, and stood there maybe a matter of five seconds, when he hopped back to the can in lee of the smoke, blinking his eyes and ruffling his feathers and obviously very proud of his bravery.

Soon he repeated the process.

The most comical part of the programme to me was the obvious screwing up of courage that was necessary each time before he took the plunge. Each time he got back out of the smoke I could almost hear him chokingly gasp to himself:

"That'll do now! This is pretty awful! You've had enough!"

But after getting his vision and breath again he seemed to be lured back for one more plunge.

For quite ten minutes he continued this off-and-on disinfecting process—for so I concluded it must be—taking about a dozen smoke-baths in all.

Finally he carefully preened every wing and tail feather in turn, before flying off with a triumphant "caw," presumably to look for a well-deserved breakfast.

But the most interesting experience I ever had with a crow was at Inverlael, by the side of Lochbroom—in 1912, as far as I can remember.

I had cycled from Strathpeffer that morning—nine miles to Garve, including the Tarvie Brae near the Falls of Rogie—and then off on the thirty-two miles to Ullapool.

It was a hot day. The long pedal up the *Direadh mòr* against what little breeze there was was pretty tiring. Then down from the top at Loch Droma—past the Coire Shalach with its well worth seeing falls, and along past Braemore and Inverbroom to Inverlael within a few miles of my destination.

At Inverlael there is another brae to negotiate. The sun was hot. I was tired and rather ahead of schedule. The lure of a grassy slope in the shade of some hazel bushes which grew between the road and the shore of the loch was too strong. Indeed that is the sort of resting-place that has a particular attraction for me. As you lie on your broad back on a warm day in a grassy glade mother earth seems to draw tiredness from your body as a blotter draws ink from paper. Half an hour of that and you are a new and invigorated man.

It was while lying there on my back and with my head in my hands that I saw the crow. I was first attracted by his peculiar form of flight. He was "towering" like a shot pheasant. Up and up and up he towered till maybe fifty yards off the ground. From there he let drop a cockle and swooped down after it. It fell on the sand and Mr Crow was at it in a second. But the cockle was still intact! That crow's face bore a most comical expression of perplexed disappointment. He cocked one eye at the mollusc, then the other, and you could practically hear him say, "Funny!"

But up he flew again with the cockle, circled round a bit and again dropped it. Down he swooped again, and again the same result. This time his expression said quite clearly, "Dashed funny!"

Up again, a wider circle, drop, swoop; nothing doing!

"Well, I'm . . . . . . !" said that crow.

But he was persistent. He picked up the cockle once again, circled wider than before, and again dropped it. Whether by chance I know not (and who dare say?), but this time the cockle fell on a patch of gravel, splitting its shell and exposing the succulent contents, which Mr Corbie soon transferred to another receptacle with gurgles of greedy delight.

If his luck was accidental he certainly had intelligence enough to profit by experience, for in the next ten minutes he picked up six more cockles and never dropped one on sand.

6

CHAPTER XIII

St Kilda Mail—Famine in the Hebrides—Landmarks in the Sound of Harris—Island Traders—Milking the *Sasunnach* "Towrists"

MORE than once, from certain vantage points in the Uists, and with the right sort of visibility, I had discerned the dim outlines of St Kilda, far away and lonely to the west: a sort of *Tir nan òg* with a magnetic pull on one's imagination. Now, while St Kilda had not been expressly included in my sphere of official operations, neither had it been expressly excluded. So there you were. *It might be my duty to go there?* Anyhow, it wasn't long before I was looking for an official excuse for a visit; nor did I have long to wait.

One spring morning a crofter on one of the smaller inhabited isles of the Uists, while bringing in seaweed, noticed a buoy floating near the shore in shallow water. Closer inspection showed it to be an inflated dog-skin to which was attached a short piece of rope, which at its other end had tied to it a small block of wood, some twelve inches long and six inches square in its other dimensions. On one side of this block, burnt in by a hot poker, were the words: "FINDER PLEASE OPEN."

The interior of the block of wood had been scooped out after the primitive boat-building plan. Several letters addressed to various people in Glasgow had been placed in the hollow. On top of these lay a note addressed: "To the Finder."

A half-inch-thick piece of wood had then been closely fitted on to form a watertight lid. This lid was with some difficulty prised open to disclose the contents of the unusual post-bag. The note to the finder was addressed and dated from St Kilda about a fortnight previously. It asked him or her to be good enough to post the other letters at the nearest post office. It also stated that there was distress amongst the inhabitants of St Kilda on account of lack of the necessaries of life.

It was my good fortune to be on that small island that day and to meet the crofter on his way home with his interesting find. As I was crossing to the mainland of North Uist that same day he asked me if I would take the buoy, box, and letters to the post office. Of course, I did; and handed the lot over to the postmaster—who gave me the interesting information that by the rules of the post office the finder of such postal packet was entitled to a reward of a half-crown. In a couple of days the newspapers were ablaze with stories of famine in St Kilda.

Let me say here and now that the "famine" report was first cousin to the report of that historical death which was said to have been greatly exaggerated. It is true that stocks of conventional necessities like tea, tobacco, and other stimulants were running somewhat low, but the starvation story (with milk, potatoes, over fifty cattle and several hundred sheep on the island) was just an audacious and astute ramp which on more than one occasion in the history of St Kilda and other Hebridean islands has brought "succour" from a credulous, kindly British public to the "starving" natives.

In this connection there was exquisite humour in the reply I once got from a native of the Hebrides in relation to one of those "famine" scares. Some newspapers went the length of publishing maps of the island with darkly shaded parts showing the daily spread of the famine! When things had grown very black indeed I met my old friend the native, and with a solemn face asked him in the Gaelic if the famine had yet reached his particular township. Well did Norman know that I knew the truth, and nobly did he rise to the occasion. His eyes twinkled through the surrounding whiskers; then a flicker of a smile and said Norman:

"Well, indeed, I am never very sure myself till I read the newspaper!" ("*Gu dearbh, cha 'n eil mi fhein robh chinnteach gus an leugh mi am paipear naigheachd.*") But this is by the way.

The day after the publication of the St Kilda famine story I wrote H.Q. suggesting that perhaps an official visit should be paid to the island. My Chief played up splendidly: it was urgent that I should go to St Kilda first opportunity. First opportunity came the following week, when the S.S. *Hebrides* called in at the pier *en route* for St Kilda on her first official call at that island since the previous September. By the way, she brought with her a Christmas mail, and I'm not yet sure whether it was meant for the previous Christmas or the next.

There were some threescore *sasunnach* holiday-makers on board. At our pier four others joined: the local excise officer, the district nurse, a native home on holiday from Canada, and myself. There was also on board MacLeod of MacLeod's factor from Dunvegan, the late Mr John MacKenzie, who was paying his annual visit to St Kilda for the purpose of collecting rents. He was a veritable mine of information regarding the island, its people and customs, and we were tremendously interested in his talk. Incidentally, he explained that rent "collecting" was somewhat of an Irishism. Actually, it was an annual settling of accounts between proprietor and tenants. The latter produced to the factor their year's harvest of oil and feathers got from some of the millions of sea-birds which frequent and nest on the island's precipitous cliffs. Each family was credited with the value of its collection of these commodities. Sometimes the value of stirks and sheep and wool was also brought in on the credit side. From the usually quite substantial total was deducted the rent—mostly under two pounds per croft —and the factor handed over the balance in cash.

We were given to understand that the independent character of the St Kildeans had of late years been sadly sapped by "tipping" and largess introduced by tourists. Formerly, young men took pride in giving gratis exhibitions of cliff-climbing. Now their amazing expertness in that direction was strictly commercialised. There was nothing much to complain of in that, but apparently the natives had become cute to the extortionate stage in the art of "milking" the *sasunnach*; and we were warned to be on guard.

The voyage out was in perfect weather. Going through the Sound of Harris—which can be navigated only in daylight because of numerous submerged rocks—was a thrilling experience. The ship was steered on lines of "landmarks" and when a new set of these came in line she would be swung hard round in less than her own length.

It was bright and sunny when we anchored in St Kilda's horseshoe bay. Out came several boats loaded with people and a great assortment of knitted garments and webs of handmade tweeds, blankets, rugs, etc. It was just like what you see at Madeira; and, believe me, the St Kildeans were no less expert traders. In the first half-hour £300 must have been transferred from the *sasunnachs*' pockets to theirs.

When it came to going ashore the Gaelic-speaking quartette got into a small boat in charge of a white-whiskered native and a youth—both wearing cheese-cutter caps. Now there was nothing in our external appearance to suggest to the boatmen that we were anything but just four of the *sasunnach* "towrists" and we never said a revealing word. The nurse had a grand sense of humour and was idolised by her patients, but it must be admitted that whatever Fate it is which confers beauty on mankind at birth must have been on vacation on her natal day. Not the most biased of fond parents could call her facially well-favoured: far, far from it! But no one knew that better than herself and little did it bother her! As we were being rowed ashore the youth sized us up with a stealthy glance and then, gazing at the sky as if discussing the weather, said to the old man:

"*Ciod e chuiridh sinn orra, saoil sibh?*" ("What will we charge them, do you think?")

The ancient then had a look at the sky and said hopefully: "*Fiachaidh sinn da thasdan*" ("We'll try two shillings")—and promptly placed his inverted cheese-cutter in front of the nurse with the announcement: "Two shillings, mem."

"Two shillings!" exclaimed the nurse in horror, and her best English accent. "What for?"

"Take you there, take you pack agaane," explained the ancient. "Chape chape too," he added.

There followed heated protests on both sides, but the nurse was adamant: she would give a shilling and not a penny more! At last the mariner gave up the unfair contest (he was at a heavy disadvantage with the language) and, speaking in his native tongue, gave vent to the cryptic soliloquy:

"*A Dhia! nach e an te ghrannd tha cruaidh!*" ("God! isn't it the ugly one that is hard!")

Retorted the ugly one: "*Ma tha mi grannd a dhuine, tha mi onarach.*" ("If I'm ugly, man, I'm honest.")

Never have I seen an island gentleman so distressed and embarrassed—and we got off for the shilling.

CHAPTER XIV

Delicate Doings—Advisory Committee—Island Wooing

In the few years preceding the date of our visit the population of St Kilda had slumped heavily. By then it was down to 79—which, by the way, was also the age in years of the oldest inhabitant—a woman. By 1930 only 39 people were left on the island, and these, at their own urgent request, were evacuated by the Government to the mainland of Scotland.

I am not, here, to go into a detailed description of our interesting six hours on the island of St Kilda, but there was a sequel so unique in my experience that it is well worth the telling.

Just before we left to rejoin the ship the then minister-cum-teacher-cum-doctor on the island (whom I had previously met in the Uists) took me aside and entrusted me with the following intriguing information. A native of the island (it will serve if I call him "Erchie"—which was not his name) was going with us on the *Hebrides* to the *Tìr Mòr* (Big Land). His mission was one of peculiar delicacy. His wife had died a few years before, leaving him with a family of very young children. After allowing him a decent interval for mourning, the old men of the island—a sort of self-elected Witenagemot, known as the "Mod," who advised on and decided all vital matters affecting the interest of the islanders—pressed strongly on Erchie the advisability of "getting someone to look after himself and the family." Erchie protested that, however desirable that might be in theory, there was the practical difficulty that every woman on the island, who might be otherwise eligible, was too closely related to himself. The Mod had been compelled to admit the validity of

Erchie's protest, but for a year now had urged the bolder step of going further afield to look for a wife. And that was what Erchie was going to do in the *Tìr Mòr*—and, wife or no wife, he must return by the *Dunara Castle*, which left him ten days for his quest. The minister, etc., suggested I might be able to help, but pleaded that I would not let the story go round amongst the *Sasunnaich* on the ship, as Erchie was anxious to avoid publicity in the matter. I promised to do my best.

Shortly after we up-anchored and left the bay I went alongside the terribly lost-looking Erchie, who brightened up visibly on being spoken to in his own tongue. First, I asked him about St Kilda. Then, I got on to the subject of his journey.

Of course, he had been to the *Tìr Mòr* before?

No, no—he had never been out of St Kilda in his life.

Oh! He would be going to the markets? Maybe to buy a cow?—or sell?

Well, well, he might be going to the markets—he wasn't very sure. Oh, yes, he might buy a cow too.

Then I tried him on domestic affairs. Of course, he would be a married man?

Och! well—yes: he *was* and he was *not*!

Och! Indeed, indeed! That was very sad. Was there a family in it?

Yes, indeed. There was; four of them—all young.

Och! Och! And who was looking after them?

Och! Indeed! Nobody but himself.

Och! Och! That was bad, bad! It was not *right*. It was not fair to the family. *He should try to get a sensible woman to look after them.*

At this stage Erchie caught me by the arm, looked round apprehensively and "*Tuiginn a so*" ("Come here"), said he, leading me away to a quiet spot near the bows. Then in a dramatic whisper: "*Eadar sinn fhein, sin mo ghnothach air an turus so*" ("Between ourselves, that is my errand on this journey").

I heartily approved the plan, and suggested that the other Gaelic speakers aboard—who knew everyone in the *Tìr Mòr*—should be let into the secret; they would certainly be helpful. At first Erchie protested against letting the cat out of the bag even to that limited extent, but ultimately he agreed.

We collected in a quiet corner of the saloon, and in our capacity of advisory committee solemnly discussed the business in hand. The Canadian—who had a strong belief in the efficacy of a dram in all critical situations in life—suggested a drop of whisky. But no! Erchie had promised the minister that he would not drink a drop of whisky while away. So we had the dram ourselves, and Erchie had a glass of "lemonade"—of peculiar sparkle. Things brightened up a bit after that. By the time we reached our port the exciseman—who naturally, with his very intimate local knowledge, became chief adviser—had prepared a list of seventeen "possibles." He wrote down not only their legal names (which wouldn't convey much to anybody) but also the names they were known by, and placed them in "order of call" as one proceeded clockwise round the island. Erchie couldn't read a word, but I have never met an apter pupil. In half an hour he had mastered the name and address of all seventeen; and that very afternoon the wooer started off on his quest. By the way, his entire "luggage" consisted of a walking-stick.

For a week there was only one topic in our island. We at H.Q. were in a fever of excitement. Every morning the postmen coming from the provinces brought in news. One day it would be "nothing doing." Next it would be two—or maybe three—wives for Erchie; but on the third day it would be back to zero again. On the seventh day

Erchie himself returned, weary and dispirited. He had called on the whole seventeen—and on a good many more —but no success! He could have a harem if he stayed on in the *Tìr Mòr* but not one would marry him and go to St Kilda; and as Erchie himself put it: "*Ciod e 's fhiach sin dhomhsa?*" ("What is the good of that to me?")

It was clearly a case for further "lemonade"—which we duly attended to. But we all felt terribly dejected, till the exciseman had a brain-wave. Why not cross by that afternoon's boat to a neighbouring island? The *Dunara Castle* called there on its way to St Kilda three days hence —and Erchie could have a three-days' hunt on fresh ground before it came. True, we didn't know so many of the "possibles" there, so the list was a short one, but you never know your luck! Inside half an hour, with hope restored, Erchie was packed off on the *Lapwing*.

It would be after six o'clock that evening by the time he could get ashore. We had made him promise to wire success or failure—indeed had provided him with the message appropriate to either eventuality—but did not expect any news till the last minutes of the last day. But after office hours that same evening down to the hotel came the Postmaster himself, with a telegram handed in less than an hour after Erchie's arrival. It read:

"Excise Officer (*Tìr Mòr*). Successful. ERCHIE."

In this tale of truth it must be recorded that we had something approaching a little spree that night.

. . . .

My colleague Archie Campbell loved the story of the St Kilda wooer, and would have it again and again. He was quite frank about the matter: he *knew* it wasn't true, but it was a good story!

Many years later *chaidh mi cheilidh air* (I went for a sociable evening) at his house in Aberdeen. When I arrived, there was a middle-aged, pleasant-looking lady sitting yarning with his wife. Mrs Archie proceeded to introduce me to the stranger. The latter smiled; there was no need for such formality: we were friends of long ago. For the life of me I couldn't place her—time and frocks fairly beat me in that way—but I did my best to hide the fact. Cautiously I went probing for firm ground:

"It's a good while since we last met," I chanced.

"It is that," agreed the lady; "it's getting on for twenty years."

"Do you know," I admitted, "I can't for the life of me remember just where it was."

"And I won't soon forget," said she. "It was yon day at *Tìr Mòr* pier when the man from St Kilda joined the boat to go to —— to look for a wife."

"*Archie !* " said I.

"Well well," admitted Archie. "*'S gu so fhein bha mi deimhinn gur e bhreug bhriagha bh'ann!* " ("And till this minute I was sure it was just a bonnie lie!")

CHAPTER XV

Storm on the Minch

THE MacBraynes steamer service to the West Coast and Islands has been so frequently the subject of popular scorn and public reproach that a defence of it requires no small degree of courage. But it is always so easy to criticise and condemn: mankind in the mass seems to have a sadistic streak which finds pleasure in that sort of talk. Yet as one with over thirty years' experience of that service, in fair weather and foul—more foul than fair —I do feel constrained to put in a warm word of respect and approbation. It is all so very easy to quote "extortionate" freights and "scandalous" conditions; but when such accusations are submitted to dispassionate investigation and analysis by any unbiased person I make bold to say that factual support for sweeping condemnation is hard to find.

Even before the day of the present fleet of miniature luxury liners—in the days (and nights) when the old *Plover* and *Lapwing*, and *Lochiel* and *Shiela*; the tiny *Cygnet* and the tubby *Handa*, and other boats of that generation, were the shuttles that ploughed their way from port to port carrying merchandise, mails, and passengers — the service was never so bad as it was painted. True, the saloon might be small, and there was no guarantee that you wouldn't find yourself rolling on its floor amongst the debris from the dinner-table which, as the result of an extra "big one," had been debunked of its broth or finnan haddies and general crockery. But MacBraynes didn't make the Minch; nor do they control the strong tides or raging gales that so frequently rouse it to furious wrath.

And the boats, if somewhat cramped, were sturdy craft of a marvellous pertinacity.

As for the men-in-charge, from captain to cabin-boy, they were a courteous, courageous breed. None so fully as they knew the thin line which so often marked the difference between "making it" and disaster; but their seamanship was superb and their courage great. May I say in passing that their successors of to-day are well maintaining the old traditions; and so far as I am concerned the only point on which I should like to be assured is that so hardy and hard-worked a class of men are adequately remunerated, and that they can look forward to a pensioned retirement from which they may in comfort look back with reminiscent pleasure on their stirring days of sailing.

One winter night many years ago I was to join the *Plover* at Lochmaddy for Lochboisdale. She was due to leave at nine P.M. and to arrive at twelve midnight. A fresh easterly breeze had blown all day. By seven o'clock it had risen sharply. By nine it looked like blowing up for a real nasty night. It was not till ten that the *Plover* berthed at Lochmaddy. When I went to go aboard Captain Black—a great little sailor—shook his head doubtfully.

"It's bad outside the loch: I was glad to get in. If it doesn't slacken soon we will have to lie here all night," was the verdict.

I confess the decision was to my liking, for the wind was playing terrifying tunes with the masts and rigging. But with an early-morning start in view it would be as well to go on board for the night. So I did.

Instead of abating, by eleven o'clock the gale had developed into a hurricane. We were storm-stayed for the night and old "Angus the Pier," after consulting with the Captain, went off to his bed.

But within an hour the unbelievable happened: with
amazing suddenness the wind died down. By eleven-
forty-five it was dead calm. A few stars appeared.

"Most extraordinary!" was the Captain's comment.
"But if this lasts for a little we'll go yet."

By contrast the calm seemed eerie; but it continued.
At the Captain's request I helped to cast off the shore
ropes, and off we slid out the loch.

Just as we passed the Big Maddy rock, and rounded
the bend to set a course down off the east coast of the
islands, the stars disappeared. From the east an ink-
black canopy came climbing up the sky. In a quarter of
an hour we were blotted out from everything as completely as if covered by a gigantic shroud and we moved
on through a Stygian night.

I was up on the bridge having a yarn with the Captain
and just thinking of turning in. Suddenly the ship
seemed to rise on top of a big wave that might be a legacy
of the gale that had so recently and so eerily died down.
But then she heeled over to starboard to such an alarming
degree that we wondered if she was going clean over.
It was when she was on the back roll from that that the
monstrous sea struck her. Later the Captain told me
it was the worst wave that had struck her in his experience.
The towering fluid monster swept across her deck as if
bent on her instant destruction.

Poor little *Plover* shivered, as a bantam boxer might
well quake on finding that he has to fight for his life
against a Dempsey. But surely a stouter-hearted bantam
never donned gloves, for, while she was as yet recovering
from the initial blow, she was struck by a sudden wind
that was as the very breath of the Furies.

Never could I get the happenings of the next eight
hours into reasonable sequence: but if the order of
events gets all mixed up in my mind the recollection of

that terrible night as a whole is vivid. The ship rolled and reared and pitched and tossed continuously; but it was when the bows got buried and the stern rose till the propeller raced in air, and all but stopped when it suddenly got a grip of the water again, or when the bow from the crest of a high wave shot upwards and then came slap down on the water, so that the ship, like a sentient suffering creature, shuddered from stem to stern, that one felt awed by the devastating powers of nature. It is doubtful if anyone on board really believed that the *Plover* could survive that terrible storm.

As the gale was from the east, the Captain's greatest concern was to steer well clear of the rocky coast to the west. So he set a course calculated to keep her well out in the Minch. Setting a course was one thing, but the extent to which the helm in that terrifying turmoil of waters could effectively impel the ship in the desired direction was a very different matter; for in addition to the disturbing strength of the water there was the problem of the immeasurable drift-effect of the wind. If only we could get one blink of the Usinish Light! But though we looked for it till our eyes ached—and we looked the whole night through—never a beam from that good light managed to pierce the awful darkness.

Not until about eight in the morning did the outline of South Uist show ever so faintly to the west; and although the sea was still running hills-high the relief which came with the certain knowledge of where we were is indescribable. For nearly eight hours now the gallant *Plover* had taken such a hammering that somehow one wanted to embrace her! Now in the light we felt cheered and confident and safe.

Meantime, in Lochmaddy, at six A.M. the Piermaster looked out of his window to confirm if the storm was as wild as it sounded. Looking in the direction of the pier he wondered why he didn't see the headlight of the *Plover*. It was pitch-dark, but the pier was only a hundred yards away. If the light was there he was bound to see it! Hurriedly Angus got into his clothes, lit his storm-lantern, and made for the pier. No *Plover*! He fought his way to the house of his nearest neighbour. The neighbour was nearly sure he had seen the *Plover*'s lights going out the loch about midnight—the wind had gone down by then. By seven Angus roused the Postmaster. The mails had been put on board last night at ten-thirty but the Postmaster understood the boat wouldn't start till morning.

Then came a telegram from Lochboisdale: Was the *Plover* still at Lochmaddy? This looked bad! The indications were that the *Plover* had left Lochmaddy at midnight; to Lochboisdale was only a three hours' run. Even making more than usual allowance for stress of weather she looked long overdue. More telegrams flew up and down the islands. The men at the lighthouse hadn't seen a sign of her! And that awful night!

Within half an hour the alarm spread. Alarm soon changed to conviction. The *Plover* was lost with all on board! Well, well! She had been a grand boat. Many's the hammering she got in her day but the Minch had beaten her at last!

But the Minch hadn't. At half-past nine, to the surprise and joy of the crowd on the pier, the *Plover* turned in to the shelter of Lochboisdale and was soon lying snug in her berth.

"A wild passage, Captain," said the hotelkeeper.

"Och, indeed! not too good," said the Captain.

CHAPTER XVI

Bride's Dilemma—Long Telegram—Happy Sequel

IN the darkening of a winter's day I pedalled along the roughish road that encircled the island. Wind as usual dead ahead, at every turn I had to stand on the crank to keep the wheels moving. Walking would have been quicker, but youthful vigour disdained that indignity. So, with ten miles to go, and a hunger that would not shrink at fried frogs, I stubbornly shoved along at something like three miles an hour.

Soon I would be passing the schoolhouse, where the restful arm-chair by the big peat fire harmonised so perfectly with the refreshing cup and cordial welcome which were the portion of all callers at that oasis. But I was in a hurry to reach journey's end and had already dealt with this temptation of the schoolhouse; firmly had I set Satan astern and was even now taking to myself full consolatory credit for that manly resolution.

Just then, all of a sudden, didn't that schoolhouse door open wide, to throw a magnetic path of light from it to my front wheel! Alas for good resolution, and *Ochanee* for human frailty! Without conscious guiding on my part if that wheel didn't turn straight for the schoolhouse door! Any chance there might have been of recovering self-respect was completely shattered by the lady teacher who now materialised in the doorway: a bonnie lassie, whose hospitality was only equalled by that of her aunt, the much-loved District Nurse, who lived with her.

But there was unwonted tension in the atmosphere of that fireside that evening. One sensed it immediately. Clearly the teacher had something on her mind; nor had the Nurse offered us one of her fund of original jokes.

"What on earth is it that's stringing you up?" I asked.

"This," said the Nurse, pointing to a huge parcel which I had already noticed.

"And what's that?" I asked, wondering.

"It's her wedding frock," said the Nurse, indicating her niece. "She is getting married in Glasgow on Wednesday of next week. The frock was made by a Glasgow firm and it arrived here by post only half an hour ago."

Of course every soul on the island knew the *Banamhaighstir sgoile* was getting married, but we were hazy about the date.

"Hooray!" says I. "Good luck! And I hope the frock is a good fit."

"That's what's bothering us," said Nurse. "From the glance we've had of it it looks on the big side—and of course we can't try it on!"

"Just that," I agreed, well knowing how unlucky a try-on of a wedding frock might be. "But surely we can have a good look at it any way."

"Certainly," agreed Teacher, loosening the strings and removing the tissue.

With trembling hands she held up the frock for our inspection. The done thing on such occasions is to exclaim "Beautiful! Exquisite!" But there was a something about that frock, evident even to a masculine eye, that forbade commendation.

"Gosh!" I gasped, "it looks bonnie enough, but it certainly does look on the big side."

"Oh! I'm sure it's far too big for me," moaned the bride, who was rather petite in her proportions. "It looks to me to be big enough for Aunty!"—with which conviction I agreed; and Aunty was *not* petite!

"Look here!" I protested. "You can't risk appearing

in that at your wedding. Circumstances are desperate, you know; you must have a try-on."

"But even if we know it's a misfit there's no time to have it put right now," she cried, loth to risk her luck.

"You would look just fine in your Harris tweed," I suggested.

But that was too much for those ceremonial days.

"Anyhow," helped Aunty, "you must try it on till we see, and we'll just chance the luck."

"Off you go, the two of you!" I urged; and the two women disappeared with the precious parcel.

In a couple of minutes or so there came from the bedroom shrieks of hysterical laughter that might easily change to weeping. Then the bride sailed in in her wedding frock. Literally, it took my breath away. It wasn't merely a misfit: it was a monstrosity. It was big enough to overlap even Aunty's ample form! A few minutes were devoted to saying things of the Glasgow firm and their precious traveller that should burn up all their ears.

The traveller, by the way, had called at the schoolhouse that same afternoon to give the soothing assurance that the frock would be by that evening's post. If only he had waited to see this awful thing! But no. He had pushed on to be in time to get across the ford. He was now on the other side and a good dozen miles away.

There are rare times when it is given to ordinary mortals to rise and shine: to overcome the impossible. "I'll have a shot at it any way," I promised; "and even if I fail you will be no worse off than you are now."

From a work-basket an inch-tape was produced. Within five minutes the Nurse and myself, working co-operatively, had taken and noted all measurements that mattered (we hoped!). In a jiffy I disposed of a substantial meal. The old Rudge was brought forth and off

I set towards the ford. There, of course, what had been dry sand two hours before was now deep in the tide. But the old postman had a boat, and knew every turn and sandbank of that treacherous ferry. The urgency of the case was explained to him—and he was game. For hours, it seemed, he piloted that boat with the sureness of a seal, finally landing me in the dark on the rocky shore on the other side. There was a mile from that rock to the beginning of the road and then five miles to the hotel where I hoped to catch up with my traveller man. Peat-bogs and ditches made heavy going as I humped the old Rudge from the rock to the road, but that night I felt like a knight of old inspired by a great resolve.

In pleasant contemplation of rest well won the traveller was ensconced in the hotel's deepest arm-chair, with a spot of comfort in a glass on a near-by table. Did he have a rude awakening! . . .

To him it was clear that a bloomer had been made in the dispatch department: the wrong frock had been sent!

Within half an hour a five-and-ninepenny telegram giving correct measurements and demanding the production without fail of a brand-new frock for the wedding morning was on its way to Glasgow. Nor—as I learned later—did the Glasgow firm let us down.

That happened a long, long time ago. Shortly after the event I met the young couple. We never happened to meet again.

But last autumn, in a Highland glen I learned that a new teacher had recently come to the school; a young lady not long qualified.

"What's the name of your new teacher?" I asked one of the youngsters. The reply threw my mind in a flash back over the years. "Can it be?" I wondered.

I would call. I did. At the schoolhouse there was an

elderly little lady with wavy white hair. "But I thought the teacher was a *young* lady!" I stammered.

"And so she is," smiled the little lady; "she is my daughter."

"Gosh! and I would know *your* voice anywhere!" said I.

"And I know yours," said she. . . .

Then her husband came in about, and for quite a while we spoke of the little school at Cladach on the island—and of an outsize in wedding frocks—and of a long telegram and its happy sequel.

CHAPTER XVII

Piloting Politicians — Halcyon Days — A Long Shower — "Butched!"—Crossing the Ferry

WHAT between the Land League activities of the eighties and nineties, the never-ending demands for roads and paths and piers and postal facilities, and the land-raiding which followed the last war, the Highlands and Islands of Scotland must have given more headaches to politicians and governments during the past half-century or so than all other parts of the realm put together. It is simply amazing how the comparative handful of electors in these fastnesses of professed liberalism and practised conservatism manage to make each successive government sit up and take notice. No doubt this mainly accounts for the fact that practically every Secretary for Scotland (or Secretary of State for Scotland, as the title now goes) has, at some stage of his tenure of that uneasy office, paid a personal visit to—as the newspapers with unfailing humourless loyalty always announced—"inquire at first-hand into the various problems affecting the Highlands and Islands." As these investigational visits usually take the form of an autumn holiday on board one of the Fishery Cruisers—a most delightful experience, as I know —it is permissible to smile at the idea of the annoyance of some future holder of that high office were he to learn that, as a result of his predecessors' efficiency, all such problems had been solved! But I hasten to assure aspirants to the office that it is a little doubtful if that joke will ever materialise.

Anyhow, it was often part of my duty—and usually pleasure—to prepare the necessary itinerary and pilot the great man safely round with a wary eye on treacherous fords and dangerous political swamps. At that time of year weather conditions were nearly always favourable. Being but human, there were times during these trips when I would have welcomed weather which would have given the visitors a conception more approximating the average of the year. Only once were my silent prayers thereanent adequately answered.

My Departmental Chief had come out to the islands to attend a series of agricultural shows. It was his first visit. He crossed a Minch like a mill-pond. He found the islands bathed in sunshine. In from the Atlantic came that warm gentle breath which shimmers in visible waves over the machairs, and sends the larks skywards in scores to pour on pedestrians their torrent of joyous song like a choral benediction from heaven.

The Chief was enchanted. What a country to live in! What a paradise! My feeble attempts at painting another side of the picture he ruthlessly brushed aside. In his view a week of that was well worth a winter of wind and rain!

Day after day, across the fords from island to island, and for nearly a week it was the same story: the same glory.

But for me it was somewhat annoying. If only he could get one real sample of the islands' weather-wickedness! But no! We crossed over to Dunvegan in an evening of unspeakable charm.

Next morning, looking out from my bedroom window I was cheered to see a mist curling down from the top of MacLeod's Tables. There was also hope in the general cheerlessness of that morning's atmosphere. Ah ha! Might I not soon have reason to chide myself for recent lack of faith in the efficacy of silent prayer?

At the door I met the Chief. He had noted the change but was not perturbed.

"There might be a few showers to-day," he informed me.

"I think there will be just one," I ventured; "but it might last all day," I added, not without a touch of genial venom. He pooh-poohed this, and reiterated that there would probably be a few showers in the forenoon but the sun should come out by midday.

We were bound that day for Kyleakin by car, and thence Kyle by ferry-boat. He took the seat of honour next Rory the driver. There he sat, a slim figure in light brown overcoat, stand-up collar and red tie, and a jaunty brown-felt hat.

I deemed it wise to don oilskin and sou'wester (which experience had advised as a routine part of the travelling outfit) and I sat in the back—and hoped and hoped.

As we started from the hotel the first big drops began to fall. At Fairy Bridge the rain no longer appeared as individual drops but as rods of water, which stotted up from the road—and from my Chief's head—with a grand ferocity. By Sligichan there was no change—unless perhaps an intensification of the downpour and of my unholy joy.

Half-way up the famous hill at Druim nan Cleochd it was still going strong. From the Chief's whiskers rivulets of water poured into his lap and were finding their way slowly but surely to the most intimate parts of his person. The road was a running burn and deeply tracked. The going was delightfully slow. As we were just about to top the summit there was a grand bang from the near rear tyre. The car stopped. Rory's announcement was brief but comprehensive:

"Butched!" said Rory.

And in very truth "butched" it was; for in those days, in the matter of providing against the possibility of *en route* repairs, Skye motor-drivers attained to the acme of optimism. A spare tyre was looked on as the last word in pessimism. The most that passengers could hope for was two or three ravaged repair outfits which between them might provide the wherewithal to patch a puncture in the inner tube. Rory ran true to type. His outfits— and an empty oil-can and some rusty levers with which he hoped in the next hour to wrench the tyre from the rusty rim—were deposited in a cavity underneath the Chief's seat. The Chief had to come to earth to let Rory get to his Pandora's box.

Oh, that lovely lingering mending! The first patch blew off as we were squeezing the cover over the rim. So we had to start all over again, including (in the absence of sandpaper) the "cleaning" of the patch-area with a mixture of spit and lucifer match. It took over an hour to complete the job, and all the time the rain continued to fall in torrents.

At Kyleakin there was a smart wind blowing and "white horses" out on the ferry. The ferryman was reluctant, but ultimately agreed to row us across. About half-way it was really rough.

Maybe the ferryman looked at me; maybe I looked at him. Maybe there was a word in the Gaelic. I can't right mind. Anyhow, the ferryman was a highly intelligent man, with skill in his job. But somehow, yon big wave took him unawares; and so it took my Chief unawares—a good half-ton of it right on his crown. And while he was still gasping for breath there came another one. The ferryman was profuse with his apologies.

I still see that drookit creature shivering on the shore at Kyle. Hat, coat, boots, and whiskers were one soaked whole. There was a gruesomely suggestive blood-red ring round his throat—but that was only the dye in the tie that had run.

CHAPTER XVIII

Moloch of Speed—Moorland Mixture—An Ardent Angler—
Troubles of a Stalker's Wife

THIS worship of efficiency and speed to which we are
now so prone has no place for praise of the more hap-
hazard and leisurely transport systems of not so many
years ago. Then, a stationmaster was master in his
station; a guard could, for a sensible friendly purpose,
stop a train off the official schedule; even a porter could
be a man, and the driver of a mail-coach wielded the
power of a commander-in-chief.

But indeed this modern craze for efficiency and speed is
only symptomatic of our attitude towards life generally.
From the cradle to the grave life is becoming a senseless
sort of sprint that is just idiotic. Mark our parental pride
and approbation when wee Johnnie cuts his first tooth a
month ahead of our neighbour's bairn!—or if he is first
to pass the "Ta-ta" or "Daddy" tape! Later, his speed
at "learning" in school is equally acclaimed. In adoles-
cent days, by common consent, his "success" is measured
by the speed with which he accumulates wealth or rank
or power. Yet when we come to shake round the
advantages to the average person of this high speed and
efficiency business we are left with mighty little in the
sieve; we may well wonder why all the hurry or where
does the real advantage come in? This speeding merely
intensifies the process of accumulating hustle; and the
necessity for hustle is one of the great delusions of the age.
Hustling! Hustling for what? "Saving time" seems
such a comical idea—as if time were in limited supply!

Yet we are all apt to be caught in the whirl. I know
a white-haired commercial gentleman who used to enjoy

a sixty-mile journey in the old mail-coach that was supposed to do the run in eight hours (but never did), or who chugged along at ten miles an hour from pier to pier (D.V. and W.P.). He now flashes from place to place in an aeroplane at 150 miles an hour and grumbles if the thing is a few minutes behind schedule. In the old days he took a friendly human interest in every house and person by the way. Even with the cats and dogs and cows he was on friendly terms. Now he has "no time"; he rushes past the interesting, friendly things in life. Soon, as a result of the ever-increasing speed of the means of locomotion, our capacity for abstracting pleasure from the contemplation of the homely things by the wayside will be lost. . . .

When resident in the far north it was sometimes necessary—or so youthful enthusiasm decided—that, in order to catch a passenger train starting at five A.M. from a station further down the line I must leave from the terminus by an overnight goods train. For the right to travel in luxury in the guard's van you had to pay first-class fare, and sign a declaration that in the event of being killed in transit you wouldn't make a compensation claim against the company. One winter's night on such a journey I was flat out and sound asleep on the hard seat at the rear of the van. A sudden stop pitched me off the seat and sent me rolling along the corrugated floor.

"What's up?" I asked the guard.

"She's stuck in the snow," he explained. "You better get up and give a hand."

We were at one of the bleakest parts of the moor: not a house within miles. Against such emergencies several shovels were carried in the van. All the available strength—driver, fireman, guard, and self—set to work on a drift quite ten feet deep. Fortunately it wasn't very long. In an hour, by the light of the moon, we made substantial inroads on the block, the engine was backed for a charge, and pouff! we were through.

Half an hour later we were jangling along about the middle of the moor. I was just dozing off again when, for no reason that I could think of—we were miles from a station—the train gradually slowed down and finally stopped. Then, of all unexpected things, the high note of a pipe-chanter with a background of dance music from a melodeon! Just at first I thought I was "hearing things," but soon there was no doubt: the music was real enough.

"What on earth is it?" I inquired of the guard, who was looking out at the van door.

"Och! just a little splore," he explained. "We are at the surfaceman's house at ——. His daughter got married yesterday and there is a bit of a dance at the house to-night. We canna pass without wishing them luck." And off out he went; and so did the driver and fireman and myself, and in we went to the cottage, that you could see only as a snow-covered mound with fiery window eyes and an open door. We got a tremendous welcome. Inside there were over a score of friends doing justice to the occasion in song and dance and feasting. Nothing would do but each of us in turn must have a dance with the bride. Fortified by generous drops of the *creutair* we had a strenuous half-hour of revelry before puffing off on the train again, and were just in time to catch up with the "passenger" at five A.M.

A favourite guard was Jimmie. He was gifted with a magnificent thirst and thrice blessed with a marvellous instinct for spotting opportunities for quenching it. The day there was nothing in your flask he just walked along the corridor giving you a cheery wave in the passing. He came in to speak to you only when there was "something doing." Just how he divined was a mystery, but he was seldom wrong, and it was seldom in the length of the train that he drew a complete blank. One such depressing day, at a remote station the train was held up for longer than usual. Passengers looked out at windows to ascertain the cause. They saw a group of railway officials, including Jimmie, gathered near the van. One had a hammer with which he solemnly tapped an axle. The driver held an "ile poorie" in his hand.

"A heated axle, but she'll be right in ten minutes," explained Jimmie to the nearest passengers. The news was passed up from coach to coach and passengers sat back resigned. I happened to be sitting opposite the gate at the side entrance to the station. Through this gate sauntered the young red-headed porter. But when he got the station between him and the train he sprinted like a hare for the hotel—some two hundred yards to the rear. In a couple of minutes he sprinted back again, came slowly through the gate and sauntered towards the group at the heated axle. They all disappeared into the van. Very soon they were out again. The driver and fireman hurried forward to the engine.

"All right now!" bawled Jimmie, for general information, and waving the green flag.

A little later he was passing up the corridor much more cheerful as to countenance.

"It's a good job you noticed it at the station," said I.

"Wasn't it?" he grinned.

As might be expected of one of Jimmie's particular gift he was an ardent angler and missed no opportunity of plying the gentle art. Against possible chances he always had with him in the van a smart little trouting rod.

The first time I saw him in action was at a certain station where a nice stream runs below the railway bridge just about where the van is when the train stops. It was a north-going train and considerably behind scheduled time.   This meant that we would have to give way to the south-coming train—not due for nearly half an hour. Some travellers went the length of saying that Jimmie manœuvred matters so that such delays must happen. Indeed I wouldn't put it past him!   Anyhow, this day he was not long in getting to work with his rod and within twenty minutes I saw him put five nice trout in the basket.

.   .   .   .

Then there was yon day the mail-coach driver stopped to collect a letter from the stalker's wife.   We found the lady in an embarrassing dilemma.   That morning her man and his fellows, with a number of terriers, had gone miles away to a *saobhaidh* (foxes' den) to try to exterminate Reynard and all his pernicious brood.   The men might not be back till to-morrow night.   At home there was a fretting infant who could not be left alone.   There wasn't a neighbour within miles.   And if that brute Molly (a rakish red cow), with the perverseness characteristic of her sex, hadn't chosen that very morning to display unmistakable and determined manifestations of an urgent desire for an amorous liaison!   The nearest entire male of her species was stanced at a farm nearly four miles down the glen.   To a stalker a calf is a calf, especially a spring calf, and for that it was already late enough in the season. Clearly, measures had to be taken.

Molly was separated from her sympathetic but futile companions.   A rope was tied round her horns.   I sat at the back of the coach grasping the other end of the rope.   The driver gathered the reins.   The stalker's wife with a supple hazel switch helped to give us a trotting start—and off we were.

Of course we couldn't go too fast, but after a while it seemed the purport of the unusual form of convoy must have dawned on Molly's intelligence, and for the last mile she put her best foot foremost with a will.

Less than a year later the driver told me he had the satisfaction of carrying, shrouded in a sugar-bag, the outcome of Molly's liaison, and that it had been sold at Dingwall for three pounds ten.

CHAPTER XIX

Reformers' Troubles—The Cult of the Pig (ancient and modern)

IT was with no little self-complacency I read over one of my early annual reports before dispatching it to headquarters. The section dealing with

SUGGESTIONS FOR SCHEMES OF WORK

AND

FUTURE DEVELOPMENTS

was particularly satisfactory. It had afforded full scope for my genius in that direction. A less biased reader might have detected in it signs of that smug arrogance which emboldens some people to make rude intrusion into the affairs of others by advocating fundamental changes in their customs, habits, and beliefs; that arrogance, for instance, which pious elderly ladies and others display in rendering financial aid to those proselytising activities which for the most part result in the questionable "conversion" of Jews or in transforming happy Hottentots into perplexed and doubtful Christians.

But such sobering reflections were to come only later. In the meantime, there was my report with its masterly survey of "defects" and of the required "remedial measures"—*Eg*.

I. In the Hebrides there was a large area of sandy loam soil, an abundance of seaweed, and a mild climate. The combination made circumstances ideal for the growing of early potatoes and other vegetables. Yet few other vegetables were grown, and not one early potato. *Ergo*, "Go to it," as the phrase now runs.

II. *Poultry.*—But for (*a*) the accident of weddings—which might involve her in a violent death and accord her an honoured place on the Hymeneal board, and (*b*) occasional disease-epidemics—which rendered her liable to a lingering death and subsequent indecent exposure and putrefaction—the Hebridean hen might hold her place on the home midden for years without number; indeed the older she grew the more firmly did she become established in the affections of her mistress. Clearly a reforming bomb must be dropped on this department.

III. *Pigs.*—Except for a pig or two at the hotels, not a pig in the place! And an abundance of potatoes and house and dairy swill going to waste!

I determined to make pigs my first concern. I recommended that three breeding sows should be placed with selected "custodians" at convenient centres. In course, piglets would be made available on such attractive terms that every crofter in the neighbourhood would be in the new industry. From small beginnings a big industry would develop. Even the necessity for a bacon-curing factory was visualised.

Unaccustomed as I then was to the strain which so revolutionary a proposal would place on the Departmental digestive system, I was much hurt when at the end of a fortnight no official approval of my pig scheme came through; indeed it didn't even receive any official acknowledgment. In a month I was enthusiastic about something else. In three months pigs had faded from my immediate outlook. Then one morning I received a telegram:

"Three farrowing sows left Oban by *Lochiel* to-day arrange with custodians."

By the way, the S.S. *Lochiel* was due to arrive at midnight, but oftener than not she would sail in around three

A.M. One of the custodians I had had in mind lived six miles from the pier, another eight, and the third a good ten miles away. Weeks ago they had given up any idea that the pigs I had spoken of would ever come. Besides, they were far from enthusiastic in the matter at any time, and sensitive as to what their neighbours would say about them. From forenoon till after dark I cycled feverishly from place to place arguing and cajoling crofters—the wives had to be won over too—to agree to take a sow and —when a grudging assent was finally extracted—helping to build suitable accommodation in the steading for the unwelcome addition to the live stock.

As per usual in such matters, news of the coming of the pigs went round the island like a broadcast. There was a record gathering that night to meet the *Lochiel*. Thank heaven, my three "custodians" had come with their carts, but they were anything but happy in their rôle of pig-pioneers and I was mortally afraid the chaffing of their neighbours would send them off home before the boat arrived. From midnight to three A.M. that night was for them and for me a nightmare of discomfort and apprehension. It required considerable liquid bribery ("closed" hours were then and there happily unknown) to keep my men till three-thirty, when Captain Mac-Dougall, after one of his worst crossings of the Minch, at long last berthed up at the pier.

The Captain met me at the top of the gangway.

"The sows . . ." I began.

"Blast the sows!" said he, with a horrible heartiness. "Squealing stubborn brutes; and one of them can go back home: her six young ones were born in the middle of the Minch. They were all dead and were thrown overboard."

"Say not a word about that on the pier," I warned him sternly. "There is plenty trouble without that!"

To the accompaniment of blood-curdling porcine protests, the terror of the horses (which had to be held by half a dozen men apiece), and the humorous comments of the crowd on the pier, each pig was put into her cart. It was ten o'clock next morning when I got back from seeing each sow established in her new home.

The fortnight that followed is one which I would fain forget. From the custodians came daily complaints. The sows' appetite was far in excess of anything they had anticipated. Then one day a telegram from No. 1 custodian demanding my immediate presence at the croft. There I was met by a distracted couple. Their sow had given birth to seven young ones but not a drop of milk had she for them! In major grunts and minor squeals old and young bewailed their lot. Neither the crofter nor his wife would keep the brutes another hour. I must take them away that very day!

Just then along came the wife of custodian No. 2. A wrathful woman! Her sow had eaten them out of house and home and still showed no signs of having any young ones. This—God forgive me!—caused me to express surprise. While I was frantically trying to extemporise a solution for this peck of troubles along came a boy on a bicycle with a message from custodian No. 3. *His* sow had given birth to nine. She had made a breakfast of five, smothered the remaining four, and was now troubled with an unwanted flow of milk!

Grateful for small mercies I collected the seven starving piglets in a box and had them straightway transferred to the now desolate and penitent cannibal, in whose milk I soused them so that the fostering was soon successfully completed. That fortuitous combination was the only bright patch in my precious plan for establishing pigs in the Hebrides. But even for the survivors there were no bidders on the island. Within a year the pigless

Hebrides were pursuing their wonted blissful way. That year, too, I came across a book written just a hundred years before my advent in the Hebrides. There had been an "improver" there then too; and he too recommended the keeping of pigs. And just as I write this—thirty years after my own disillusionment—I have officially submitted to me "for observations" a report from the present-day Agricultural Organiser in the Hebrides—and *he* sees a great future for pigs there! Good luck to him!

CHAPTER XX

As a good character and repute are as desirable in a crofter as in a king, the selecting of a tenant for one of our holdings always caused me much concern. It was while questing for confidential and reliable information regarding an applicant for a holding that I received from an old native the mystifying reply:

"*Och! Faodaidh e bhi mar sud no mar so, ach gu dearbh cha chuala mise riamh gu do chaill aon de'n t-seorsa sguab as an t-sugain*" ("Och! he may have his good points and his bad; but indeed I never heard that one of his kind ever lost a sheaf from the *sugan*").

Here, clearly, was the retort parabolic, but it was a new one on me; so I asked for light.

"Och," said he, "it is just a way we have here of speaking well or not so well, but at least truthfully, of a man according to the reputation of his forebears."

"But what is the whole story?" I asked, keen for light on darkness. So we sat for an hour on the *garadh-fail* (feal dyke) while the old man expounded the intricacies of a highly developed communal system that is as interesting as it is instructive. The system was still in full operation in his township and in some of the others, but it worked so smoothly that an outsider might live on the island for a lifetime and never know anything about it. Here is my attempt at the picture.

On most estates in the Hebrides the subdivision is mainly of the "township" nature. A township comprises an irregular number of crofts whose tenants in addition to having individual lands have common use of certain

areas. In the township which the old man described to
me the croft was made up of a share in three different
areas of land, in addition to the land held in individual
occupation. The three shared lands were:

Machair (sandy land near the sea);

Geàrraidh (superior pasture-land for milch cows);

Monadh (hill pasture for sheep).

The individually occupied *Dubhthalamh* (black or loamy
land) was where his house and steading were built, and
came in between the *Machair* and the *Geàrraidh*.

The *Machair* is the flat sandy land (though sometimes
broken with bent-covered sand-dunes) which lies between
the seashore inwards to where the *Dubhthalamh* begins.
A dyke or fence roughly parallel with the shore separates
Machair from *Dubhthalamh*. The *Machair* (which may
extend to several hundreds of acres) is subdivided into
large fields. A field is known as a *sgat*. On each *sgat*
there are as many rigs as there are crofts in the township. Always, two or three or more *sgats* are in cultivation. After bearing crops for two or three years in
succession the *sgat* is allowed to rest for some years. It is
not sown out to grass but left to natural regenerative
processes. By the end of a year or two it will be well
covered with a variety of more or less useful pasture
plants.

It follows that each year a *sgat* will fall due to be left
out of cultivation and that another which has been long
rested must be brought into cropping. At the beginning
of winter the township "Constable" calls a meeting of all
the tenants to decide which *sgat* should be thus brought in.
The Constable, by the way, is one of the crofters who has
been appointed by the *Bàilidh* (Factor) as his local agent.
After the *sgat* for cultivation has been decided on there
is a meeting on the ground to allocate to each man his
rig. This is done by a form of double ballot. The rigs

are numbered. For the first draw the Constable puts papers in his hat numbered up to the number of tenants. The men approach the hat for the first draw not in any regular order. But that draw is only to decide the order in which each man will approach the hat for his second draw. It is the number on his second paper that determines the number of his rig.

This rig is his until that *sgat* is left to rest again two or three years hence; and from the moment that his lot is known his main concern in life seems to be the manuring of that rig. Throughout the winter and spring, in fair weather and foul, he is cutting and collecting and carting incredible quantities of seaweed on to it. There is sharp, all-round rivalry as to who will get the best crop out of his rig. The effect, in early autumn, when two or three *sgats* of maybe thirty acres each are bearing beautiful crops of barley, potatoes, *coirce-beag*, or rye, is very impressive indeed; and the stately herds of Highland cattle as they move with majestic leisure, grazing over the pastures of the *Machair*, complete a remarkable scene of rural beauty and peace.

Lying inland from the *Dubhthalamh* is the *Geàrraidh*, with its rich pasture, where the milk cows are summered. From the day they are put out to the *Geàrraidh* till the approach of winter they never enter a byre. Each evening, after milking, they are driven into the *buaile* (a spacious stone-built enclosure or fold) by the *buachaille* (herd), who lets them out again for milking in the morning.

Buachailleachd is often an hereditary job. As part of his remuneration he occupies, rent-free, a small house and croft within the township. During the summer and autumn when all the cows are out at pasture—and there may be well over a hundred of them to look after—the *buachaille* is provided with a daily assistant. This assistant —often a lad or an old man or woman—must be supplied from each house in the township in turn. On Monday the assistant will come from No. 1 house; on Tuesday from No. 2, and so on, right round and round every croft till the end of the season. The croft from which the assistant comes has also on that day to give the *buachaille* his dinner. As may be surmised, than the *buachaille* there is no sounder judge of the standard of culinary skill amongst the housewives of the township!

One of the sights of the islands is the morning and evening trek to the milking. In the morning each family group of cows, recently released from the *buaile*, hangs around looking with expectant eyes for the coming of the mistress, who sometimes brings the gift of a specially succulent titbit, in return for which—and bewitched by a Gaelic song—"*Ciabhag*" cheerfully acquiesces in the theft of her progeny's birthright. After milking, each cow strolls off to begin that almost never-ending foraging that will ensure filled pails again in the evening.

The number of cattle a crofter may keep is regulated by his "souming"—usually expressed in cows, or *cailep*, which is the eighth part of a cow. Thus if the "souming" for a croft is 8 cows, that equals 64 *cailep*. A three-year-old beast equals 6 *cailep*; a two-year-old 4, and a one-year-old (or stirk) 2 (calves are "off the coupon"); and so long as he does not exceed his total souming a man may make up his stock in any way that suits him best. For instance, on such a place he would probably have:

$$
\begin{array}{lll}
5 \text{ cows} \times 8 & = 40 \text{ } cailep \\
1 \text{ three-year-old} \times 6 = & 6 & ,, \\
2 \text{ two-year-olds} \times 4 = & 8 & ,, \\
5 \text{ stirks} \times 2 & = 10 & ,,
\end{array}
$$

Total   <u>64 *cailep*</u>

Bulls were supplied from the big-farm folds, of which

in those days there were some very good ones. No money passed. The farmer loaned the bull to the township in return for a specified number of days' work to be provided by the crofters at harvest, peat-cutting, sheep-smearing, etc.

The wintering of the bull was also an obligation on the township. At the end of harvest a meeting was held to decide whether the crop that year was a big one, a poor one, or a middling one. On that decision depended the daily ration of the bull throughout the winter: he was fed in accordance with the bountifulness (or otherwise) of Providence.

The exact measure of the bull's big, little, or medium ration was governed by the *sugan*. The *sugan* was a short rope made of pleated bent-grass. It had a loop at one end. Towards the other end there were three knots, each about six inches from the other. The obligation to provide the day's ration for the bull fell on each crofter in the township in turn. Each evening, to-day's supplier would pass on the township *sugan* to to-morrow's supplier. The ration was in the form of sheaves of *coirce-beag*. The *sugan* was stretched on the ground. Sheaves were laid on it to the number which would allow of the burden being tightened by the *sugan* to the appropriate knot for that year. But, as everyone knows who has tied a burden in that fashion, the degree of security of the load will depend on the degree of tightness of the rope. Therefore, when loop and knot met, if the burden was still loose— in other words, if you hadn't put enough sheaves in (or more plainly still, *if you were trying to cheat the bull*)—the chances were that some of the sheaves would fall out before you reached the bull-house with your burden. What clearer evidence of mean dishonesty and disgrace: *you had lost sheaves from the sugan*. And so to this day in the island a man is well spoken of (or not so well) according as his forebears were honest (or not so honest) with the feeding of the bull.

"Now," concluded the old man, "you will understand my answer to your question about Norman: 'Och! he may have his good points and his bad; but indeed I never heard that one of his kind ever lost a sheaf from the *sugan*.'"

CHAPTER XXI

The Magic-lantern—High Jeenks—A Sheep and a Lamb—
Controlling the Shebeen

LITTLE did I dream, as I waited for the mail gig in the dark and wet and wind of that March morning, of the stirring time which was waiting for me round the corner. "Round the corner" is really a figure of speech, though; for there were seventeen miles to travel to the ferry in yon hideously plain and battered dog-cart that on alternate days carried His Majesty's mail to the outposts; and then a two hours' row in a boat before I would reach my destination—and, as it happened, the locus of an unexpected experience.

Meantime (six A.M.) at the town post office the angular "shalt" that supplied the motive power for the dog-cart champed his bit and did some semi-prancing that might have encouraged a stranger to think he would make short work of the miles once he got a-going. I was saved that pitfall, for well I knew how soon the initial burst of speed would slacken to a sober trot that would so readily come to a dead stop on the slightest prospect of a wayside gossip. Most of the way it was that jog-jog, jog-jog, jog-jog which only the combination of a slow-trotting horse and an ill-balanced dog-cart can produce. By the end of the second hour you felt that the eternal nid-nid-nodding of your head was seriously threatening your mental equilibrium and your one comforting reflection was the knowledge of the rousing effect on your liver. With the exception of restful minutes at road-ends, where there were exchanges of courtesies and news, and the driver was entrusted with a variety of commissions, this physical-jerks process continued during the four hours which the old horse took to do the seventeen miles to the ferry. To add to the charms of the drive, business-like showers of sleet came pelting along every half-hour or so. It takes a very special arrangement of rugs and oilskins to success-fully resist such sleety onslaughts, and I know of no more dismaying moment than that in a dog-cart when you suddenly realise that all your careful sartorial dispositions for securing immunity for your person have failed: that even now your posterior is in direct and chilling contact with a pool of ice-cold water!—and that there are still many miles to go!

When we emerged refreshed from the ferry-house we were gladdened by a decided improvement in the day. It looked as if a whimsical Weather Clerk, regretting his earlier scurvy treatment of us, was trying to make amends. He succeeded too; and the row down the loch in the shelter of a friendly island was in genial sunshine.

At the landing-jetty a small crowd of young men were waiting. Even before we landed they shouted to ask if I had brought my magic-lantern with me. This lantern, by the way, had proved an excellent "draw" at lectures; but as it happened I hadn't brought it on this journey. It was only when the situation was fully explained that I understood the keen disappointment which this omission caused amongst the lads on the jetty. Here was their story.

Two months previously the younger spirits in the township had decided that, as one item in a general effort to raise funds for a cattle-show, a concert should be held. But never in history had a concert of any kind desecrated that stronghold of Calvinism. The daring promoters got their first rebuff when the local school-management committee, headed by the minister, refused them the use of the school. Also there had been some pointed pulpit references to the "freevolities of the rising generation."

Somewhat daunted, but wholly determined, the lads applied to the School Board, who, greatly daring, granted them the use of the school in face of the local ban. But this had caused delay. The concert, which had been fixed for a date early in February, had to be postponed. It was now timed to take place on the very evening of the day of my arrival. But alas! feared by the frown of the Church, most of those who had been depended on to contribute songs and music had asked to be excused. Defeat was staring the committee in the face. Then came a hope when they heard that "*Fear an ìm*" ("The butter man"—I used to lecture on butter-making) was coming and that he might be bringing his magic-lantern— now of considerable local renown. They had telegraphed the previous evening asking me to be sure to bring it— but now realised that the telegram could not possibly be delivered before I left that morning. The position was desperate. Would I send a telegram at once to instruct that the magic-lantern be sent to the ferry by special hire that day? They would themselves boat it in good time from the ferry.

There was only one thing to do; and it was done. Moreover, unlike some island last-minute efforts of that nature, there was no disappointment: the magic-lantern did arrive in good time to take an honourable place at a memorable concert.

Meantime, local excitement was running high, the pro- and anti-concert elements doing their respective bests. For better or worse I, of course, was in the camp of the former.

"What sort of a programme are you hoping to get together?" I inquired (an hour before the concert was billed to commence) of the Secretary, a genial giant with a noble contempt for ministerial inhibitions.

"There's no programme at all yet; but och! we'll

soon make a programme when we see who turns up,"
said this optimist.

At eight P.M. the Chairman, Secretary, members of
Committee, and myself, accompanied by a band of
enthusiastic supporters, set out to walk the two miles to
the school—this with a charming indifference to the
announcement in the handbills: "Doors open at 7 P.M.
Concert begins at 7.30."

We arrived at eight-forty-five to find the school in total
darkness. The schoolmaster was in the opposition camp,
so merely left the school door unlocked. We lit the
solitary hanging lamp. Not a sign as yet of an audience,
but that caused no concern to the officials.

"They'll turn up all right before ten o'clock, you'll see,"
declared the secretary.

He was right: at about nine-thirty voices and footsteps
were heard approaching. Within ten minutes a very
large crowd had gathered at the door. Meantime,
dispositions had been made for dealing with the two
essentials—taking the money and preparing a programme.
I was entrusted with the former duty and collected the
shillings as fast as I could allow the people to pour in.
It was a simple cash-down business. I just threw the
money into an enamel milk-basin set on a near-by table.

The Chairman and Secretary (with the unsolicited
assistance of ardent but not always unanimous advisers)
prepared the programme. Their *modus operandi* was
delightfully simple. The Secretary, with a double foolscap
sheet of paper and pencil in hand, stood inside the
door. The Chairman stood beside him acting as chief
spotter. Every time he saw a likely artiste passing in he
whispered to the Secretary to add that name to the rapidly
increasing list of victims, who were as yet in complete
and blissful ignorance of the honour conferred upon them.

By ten o'clock the big classroom was filled from its

back wall to within a desk-breadth of its inner side. In triumph the Secretary produced to the Chairman and myself his programme. The list of names extended over nearly two pages of foolscap: over seventy names in all. I ventured the opinion that that was on the big side: that indeed half that number would be more than enough.

"Och! we'll soon sort that, then," said the indomitable Secretary; and straightway, with a blue pencil, he proceeded ruthlessly to obliterate more than half of the names whose owners had so nearly but unwittingly attained to local fame. The names so summarily blotted out were of those judged to be less efficient performers, but the final list was not adjusted without some considerable differences of opinion amongst the small coterie of self-appointed advisers—who succeeded in getting one or two "reprieves." But in regard to a certain Donald MacLeod whose name had suffered blue-pencil extinction, when one admirer protested that the name should be left in because he (the admirer) had recently heard the same Donald sing beautifully at a certain wedding, the evidence was summarily rejected.

"Just that," agreed the Secretary: "very likely he would do well enough at a wedding but he's much too sober for to-night."

At ten-thirty everything was in readiness for a beginning with the concert. It was now the Chairman's turn to shine; and he did, spiritually and physically. He was a delightful old man with the heart of a lad of twenty. With singular independence he had scorned the carping criticisms of his coevals and given wholehearted support to the concert. There he stood now, rather tightly encased in his wedding suit of many many years ago. The coat had yon elusive pocket secreted in its tail. He had much difficulty in extracting from this hidey-hole a large-sized handkerchief needed frequently and urgently for wiping his profusely perspiring brow. His whitening beard still showed streaks of its pristine red. Normally his cheeks were of fresh and youthful colour: to-night, partly as a result of unwonted excitement—and partly no doubt as a result of frequent visits to the little class-room where a supply of liquid refreshment for the Committee and a few other privileged people had been cached —they shone like American apples, and his whole countenance radiated geniality all round.

Prompt at ten-thirty he got up to make his opening remarks. There was a gloriously defiant challenge in his voice and eye:

"Ladies and Gentlemen. Here we are at last, all ready to begin the first concert in the history of this parish. I am very pleased to see such a grand turn-out and I'm not going to say a word about those who ought to know better than to be in opposition to this concert. But I am glad to see that so many have more sense than those who are supposed to be their betters.

"And now the first item on the programme is a tune on the bagpipes by Johnnie Murray."

"No! No!" interposed the Secretary. "Johnnie was to come to the first concert but he was afraid to turn up to-night."

"What!" exclaimed the inspired Chairman. "I am not going to say a word about those who ought to know better than to be in opposition to the concert, but I cannot let the concert start without a piper."

"But there is no piper here, man! Just make a start with a Gaelic song and it will do fine," urged the Secretary.

"Never!" retorted the implacable Chairman. "I am not going to say a word about those (etc. etc.) . . . but if we start without a piper they will think we were afraid."

There was some desperate talk of sending some of the lads down to the Lodge (over two miles away) to see if the gamekeeper could be induced to come with his pipes; but it transpired that the keeper was from home.

The impasse was complete, so I whispered to the Chairman that if only we could get a set of pipes I would try to give them a tune myself and let him get on with the concert.

"What!" ejaculated the astonished autocrat. "Can you play the pipes?"

"Only a little and not very well," I protested, "but it would let you get on."

He was on his feet in a jiffy: "Ladies and Gentlemen. I am not going to say a word about those who should know better than to be in opposition to this concert, but we must begin the concert in proper style with the bagpipes. I am sorry to say our own piper has not turned up to-night, but we are very fortunate in having with us our good friend Mr MacDonald who is an old hand at the pipes, and he will give us an opening tune. The pipes are down at the keeper's. Three or four of you boys there run down, like good lads, and get them here as quick as your legs will carry you. The men can light their pipes and have a smoke or make love to the lassies till the boys come back."

On the instant (eleven P.M.) half a dozen youths ran off over the moor in the direction of the keeper's house—where, it was surmised, the wife would still be afoot.

The principal "officials," including the prospective piper, repaired to the little classroom. Perhaps it was an illusion associated with this visit to the classroom, but anyway it did seem to me the boys hadn't been more than ten minutes gone when they were back with the pipes. A preliminary trial assured me that the pipes, though lacking tartan bag-cover and drone ribbons, were all right in the essentials. Again, the little classroom may have had something to do with this, but I do really believe that

9

at that midnight hour, to open the concert I played as I never played before—nor since. Of one thing I have no doubt at all: never did I receive such an ovation.

The Chairman was riotously triumphant. He was not going to say a word, etc. . . ., "but that was a grand opening to the concert. The next item on the programme is a Gaelic song from——"

He peered through his spectacles but failed to decipher the name. Then, for the first time, everybody noticed that the single paraffin lamp was smoking so badly that the globe was black with soot. It was also discovered that the globe was cracked, so that cleaning without breaking it was out of the question. There was only one thing that could be done: the wick was screwed down, and we were left in all but complete darkness. But the Chairman, whose rosy countenance now reflected what little light there was, brushed the lamp incident aside as too trifling a matter to dim the happiness of great minds. By the light of a match he and the Secretary scrutinised the programme and agreed that the first item was due by Miss Mary MacLeod. But the point wasn't so easily settled as that: there happened to be several ladies of that name present and each one of them was now being urged by her immediate neighbours to step forth and sing. All of them refused the honour in quite emphatic terms. The ambiguity was removed only by the Chairman's explanation that the lady whose name was on the programme was Mary, the daughter of Donald, the son of Angus, the son of Big Malcolm. On that the persuasive efforts of the whole audience were concentrated in the direction of this highly honoured but embarrassed young lady. Her protests were of no avail. Out she had to go, propelled towards the floor by many muscular arms. But sing she did, naturally, easily, sweetly, one of those haunting Gaelic songs that go so near to making a bairn of a grown man. She was encored twice—and so, for that matter, was every one of the other singers; who, by the way, were announced in similar fashion and made similar initial protests against the unexpected honour. But the concert was now in full swing and going merrily.

By four A.M. we were well down towards the finish of the first half of the programme; but we were destined never to hear the rest of it, for just then the Chairman had an inspiration which would make a mere concert pale into insignificance as a red rag to those who ought to know better . . .

"Ladies and Gentlemen," he announced, "I am not going to say a word about those who ought to know better than to be in opposition to this concert, but I am sure that you will agree with me that we have had a most enjoyable evening so far [*loud cheers*] and now, as it is as well to be hanged for a sheep as for a lamb, I propose that we have a DANCE."

This startling announcement was greeted with frenzied cheering. In five minutes the seats were piled up at one end of the room. In less than another minute the floor was crowded with couples all set for a reel, with the Chairman and his lady at the top end. The piper was perched on top of the teacher's high desk and—*Hooooch!* they were off.

The dancing was the heartiest and most strenuous I had ever seen; and through it all that prince of diplomatists, that most dauntless of leaders, the Chairman, was a sight for the gods of Mirth as he stepped and stamped and swirled, hooched and mopped up the perspiration with the large handkerchief—which now for convenience was partly jammed inside the waistband of his tight wedding trousers and partly floated like a victory banner when he did an extra quick whirl.

This was no paltry dance-and-rest affair. Every couple

danced to the point of physical exhaustion, and when they sat down to recover, others, fiercely fresh, joined in. There was no respite for the piper, who played for a solid hour and a half. Fortunately, at nearing six A.M., he was relieved by a fiddler, who by the spiritual intoxication of the dance was emboldened to play.

With a throat like a smiddy file I headed for the wee classroom—only to learn that the supply had gone done half an hour ago. It was a bitter blow! But the Secretary suggested that if I went outside and saw the policeman he might be able to save my life. I soon found the guardian of the law and hinted to him that piping was hard on the throat. He led the way to yon usually unused little building that stood in a corner of the country school playground. He squeezed his ample form in past the door. I followed. With a match the policeman lit a stump of candle fixed in a bottle set on an up-ended beer-box. There was plenty plenty more too. Just for company the policeman bar-tender had one or so with me. Then I heard him murmur something about "two shillings" but didn't just catch the drift.

"That will be two shillings," he said now quite pointedly. He then explained that the Committee's supply was free but that on this side-line they were trying to make a little for the concert funds—so the control had been placed in the safe hands of himself!

"Of course, of course; just that," I agreed, as I handed the cash to the constituted authority, and returned to the revels in the school.

The morning lights were high in the east when tired but triumphant we skailed our ways homeward.

PART III

CHAPTER XXII

The Lure of Lewis

THE island of Lewis seems to possess an irresistible attraction for "improvers." Again and again in the course of its history it has been bought or invaded by people who seem to have discerned in its somewhat sterile exterior possibilities of profitable development or exploitation. In the seventeenth century a syndicate of Fifers—who came to be known as "The Fife Adventurers"—made ambitious plans for the exploitation of Lewis, but soon found themselves in such a hot water of native opposition that ultimately—and not without considerable bloodshed—they were compelled to abandon their project and quit the island.

At a later period Sir James Matheson, a wealthy Eastern merchant, bought Lewis. Sir James made earnest and costly endeavours to improve social conditions by reclaiming land, establishing industries, developing the fisheries, etc., but with such meagre success and at such heavy cost that in the long run he had no alternative to throwing in the towel—having all but bankrupted himself in a most gallant fight.

The latest victim of the Lewis allurement was Mr T. B. MacAulay, a wealthy Canadian with genealogical roots in "Eilean an Fhraoich" ("Isle of Heather"). Inspired by a mixture of loyalty and sentiment Mr MacAulay some years ago fostered and financed a sustained effort to demonstrate the practicability of scientifically reclaiming the peat-land of which Lewis has so large an area, so that it might grow profitable crops instead of only rather inferior pasture. How far this effort has succeeded I am not to say. Certainly, surprisingly good crops have been made to grow on the MacAulay peat farm, but at what cost seems somewhat obscure. Beyond doubt the cost was big; the "reclamation" is doubtfully permanent. Incidentally, it may be explained that most of the arable land in Lewis had already over the centuries been reclaimed from peat by the slow but simple process of removing for fuel all but a little of the peat, which was then mixed with the underlying clay to form a not-too-bad crop-growing medium. This laborious but interesting process of "skinning" the land of peat and then preparing it for crops is still to be seen in operation: it is fairly common to see the year's requirement of peat drying on the "bank" of the hag while a crop of potatoes or oats is growing alongside in the bottom of the hag from which last year's peat was taken. Reclamation by this process is certainly slow but it has the merit that it doesn't cost cash; "elbow grease" and time are the two essentials— and in normal years there is a good deal of both available in Lewis.

But the most spectacular of all the Lewis "improvers" was the late Lord Leverhulme. The great industrial magnate had again and again proved his remarkable genius for successful business enterprise. Towards the end of the 1914–18 War I suspect he found himself in the same dolorous plight as the great Alexander with no more worlds to conquer. Inactivity to a man of Lord Leverhulme's dynamic personality was intolerable. Then, by some chance, Lewis began to attract him—as it had so many others. The more he studied the fishing industry out there the more he was intrigued by its tremendous scope for organisation and expansion; so he bought the island.

Now Lewis, as usual in time of war, had contributed an astonishing number of men to the fighting forces. Those —or what were left of them, for the toll was cruel—were being demobilised at the time their island passed into the new ownership. The first reaction of the natives to the news was one of hopeful anticipation. What could not a wealthy proprietor do to help settle them in crofts on their beloved island?

To a materialistic outsider seeing a typical Lewis croft for the first time this agricultural unit might well appear but a miserable affair. But how far, far wrong he would be in that estimation! To a Lewisman that croft is the most precious spot on earth: to it he is bound by a thousand ties of memory, sentiment, and HOME. For, wherever he may go in pursuit of wealth or fame, or even for a mere livelihood—and they are world-wide travellers —in his heart of hearts there is only one HOME: that little house with its few acres of land in Eilean Leodhais.

This intense love of the Lewisman for his island home is told in that inexpressibly beautiful Gaelic song *Mo Dhachaidh* ("My Home")—a verse or two of which are rendered somewhat freely on the following page.

Imagine therefore the consternation of the returning warriors when the rumour went round that the new proprietor was set dead against making any additional crofts on the score or so of still remaining large farms. Their first hopeful anticipation gave place to strong and angry resentment. Meetings were held in every principal township on the island, from which emphatic resolutions were forwarded to the Government demanding the break-up of the farms into crofts; and threats were not lacking that, failing legal sanction, forcible possession would be resorted to.

The reason for the new proprietor's refusal to countenance the formation of additional crofts lay in his honest

Doh is E♭

```
{ :s .f | m :-.d :d | d :-.m :s | d' :t :l | s :- }
  My    | heart it is  buoy-ant, my | steps gay and  free,

{ :f | m :-.d :d | d :r :m | f :m :f | r :- }
  At  | close of the day, as I | steer straight for thee,

{ :f .f | m :-.d :d | d :-.m :s | d' :t :l | s :- }
  Where the | love of my life  and my | bairnies a - glee,

{ :f | m :d :m | r :t₁ :r | d :- :- | d :- ||
  Are | waiting to welcome me | home—      HOME.

{ :d .d | d :-.r :m | m :-.m :m | s :-.m :m | m :- }
  What are | tur - ret-ed cas - tles and | dwellings so  grand,

{ :m | f :-.m :f | r :-.m :f | s :m .:d | d :- }
  To  | one who was reared in yon | cot by the strand?

{ :s | l :-.f :f | d' :t :l | s :f :m | d' :- }
  Yon | snug but and ben with its | wee plot of land,

{ :f .f | m :d :m | r :t₁ :r | d :- :- | d :- ||
  Is my | palace,  my  lode-star, my | heart - - home.
```

My heart it is buoyant, my step gay and free,
At close of the day, as I steer straight for thee,
Where the love of my life, and my bairnies aglee,
Are waiting to welcome me home—HOME!

*   *   *   *

Away the false pleasures of wine cup and gold!
So transient, so sordid, so shallow, so cold,
Compared with the uplift, the rapture untold,
That streams in the beam from thy window.

*   *   *   *

My heart, etc.

conviction that crofts were "uneconomic." In face of threatened land-raiding he was assiduous in efforts to explain this to the people, in the hope of getting them to agree with his view that under an industrial régime they would be much better off. At the Castle he gave a series of dinners and entertainments to which he invited in relays most of the influential people of the island. But, whatever degree of success attended this stratagem, the demand of the returned soldiers and sailors was overwhelming and insistent. Raiding broke out in several centres; soon the island was in a ferment.

One day in the north, when I read in the *Scotsman* of the trouble in Lewis, with a shrewd instinct for self-preservation I tried to get officially "lost" in the wilds of Sutherlandshire. But a rascal of a telegraph messenger—a really bright lad—proved too efficient. With untiring tenacity he tracked me to my hidey-hole to deliver the inevitable yellow envelope which contained the curt instruction to proceed to Lewis immediately!

There was the usual crowd on Stornoway pier next night, awaiting the arrival of the *Shiela* (now mouldering in the bed of the Minch whose wild waters for so many years she so gallantly rode). Many of those on the pier were old friends and soon I was generally spotted as "the man from the Board." Questioners in Gaelic and English demanded to know what the Board were going to do. I evaded the point as best I could; I could not say anything until I got my instructions.

Next morning I called at the post office for instructions, but found none!—and let me say now that during the whole of that six-weeks' stay the divil a guiding instruction did I get! No doubt there were good reasons for this policy of silence but it was mightily embarrassing for the official on the spot, and made him feel an awful ass.

Would the Board back Lord Leverhulme in his industrial schemes—which ruled out the prospect of any additional crofts—or would they use the power they had to provide crofts for the returned soldiers and sailors? It was an answer to that question which was demanded of me by emissaries of both sides who came in force to see me during the next week. Easier asked than answered!

As I write this, at a time when the mightiest armed conflict in the history of the world is raging round diametrically opposed human ideals, the trouble caused to a landlord and to the British Government of twenty years ago by the natives of an island in the Hebrides in demanding the right to live "freely" on the land in preference to a life of "servitude," which industrialism threatened to impose upon them, may seem a trivial matter. Yet I believe there is a direct relationship; that the urge for "freedom" (and what life is so free as that on the land?) which actuated Lewismen then is of the very essence of the great urge which now animates the opposition to Hitlerism; and that even in that little struggle in Lewis there lies a lesson for our statesmen of the future.

CHAPTER XXIII

Meeting with Raiders—Greek meets Greek—The Philosopher—
Bodach an t-siapuinn—The Optimist

THE atmosphere into which I stepped off the *Shiela* that night at Stornoway was highly charged. From the Army, the Navy, and the Mercantile Marine hundreds of men had already returned to the islands, hundreds more would be demobilised soon (hundreds, alas! would return only with MacCrimmon). The lads had been led to believe that crofts would be ready for them. Not only were there no crofts ready, but with a hostile proprietor, and a hesitant Government, their prospects of being settled on the land were anything but bright. Disappointment, succeeded by intense anger, surged through the island. Just before my arrival mere threats of raiding had developed into reality. Land-raiding became general. In one case there were three raids in two days on the one farm. The new factor (from England) was thoroughly scared. Lord Leverhulme appealed to the Government for the protection of the law. The returned soldiers appealed to the Government to have the farms broken up immediately. The Press revelled in the situation, and the whole atmosphere became electrical and highly embarrassing to the Government and the Scottish Office. It was at this juncture that I received instructions by wire to proceed to Stornoway immediately.

It is not to be inferred that here was a case of the silent strong man being called upon to extricate the Government from its difficulties. The simple fact is that a representative had to be on the spot, and I was selected merely because I was the one of the staff who happened to know Lewis best, and its language; and I went in anything but heroic spirit. Yet I am grateful for being privileged to have taken an intimate (if somewhat futile) part in the Lewis Drama of that time, because of the intensely interesting insight it afforded of the views and motives which actuated the protagonists. For it was intensely interesting; and if I succeed in passing on to others even a little of that interest and pleasure I shall be very glad.

It was indeed no easy matter for the Government to decide on any active course. If they decided to break up the farms Lord Leverhulme would abandon all those schemes which, if brought to fruition, might bring hitherto undreamed prosperity to Lewis. On the other hand, if they decided to support Lord Leverhulme by refusing to break up the farms they were up against the fact that the returned soldiers were in illegal possession and that nothing short of armed force would compel them to quit. It was in very truth a dilemma. But this is digression, and I am mainly concerned to tell the story of the meeting between Lord Leverhulme and the raiders.

Lord Leverhulme called to see me one morning. He was my first millionaire and Industrial Magnate and I shall not soon forget the occasion. At very first glance one would put him down as a rather insignificant little fellow. That impression lasted for a shorter time than it takes to write it. Charm, tact, decision, power radiated from the man's every word, look, and gesture. I had never met a man who was so obviously a megalomaniac and accustomed to having his own way. He had the sort of personality which immediately afflicts ordinary people with a pronounced inferiority complex. In these circumstances I realised that I must adopt one of two courses straight away: either accept the position and become submissive to the strong will; or make instant and silent appeal to the shades of my forebears to grant me strength to still retain at least a little of my own individuality—indicating a sort of resentment! I adopted the latter alternative and am consoled to think my appeal was not quite unheard.

After just the right amount of greeting and tactful flattery Lord Leverhulme informed me that he had arranged an open-air meeting with the raiders at eleven o'clock to-morrow and would like me to go along with him to the farm. I had no wish to go to the meeting and said so plainly. But he pressed that I should go. I would not go.

"Pity," said he, making for the door, "but I hope you will change your mind. Good-bye." Within three hours I received a telegram from H.Q. instructing me to attend the meeting. Almost immediately afterwards Lord Leverhulme reappeared.

"Well," said he, "have you changed your mind?"

"I have," said I.

"Good," he grinned, "I thought you would. I'll call for you in my car at ten-thirty to-morrow morning."

"Thanks," I grinned back, "but you needn't trouble. I'll have that much of my own way, and I'll go in one of Kenny Henderson's cars."

"All right: that must do. Good-bye," and off he went.

To-morrow at the farm steading we found over a thousand people gathered for the meeting; mostly men, but there was a fair smattering of women. It was a sullen crowd, resentful of the situation which had developed. One wrong note might have precipitated serious trouble. But no wrong note was struck; and if Lord Leverhulme sensed any danger he certainly showed no sign. He walked right into the middle of the crowd, made a little "ring" for himself and his interpreter, mounted an upturned tub (in which the farmer was wont to brew a real knock-me-down brand of beer), raised high his hat, smiled genially all round and said:

"Good morning, everybody! Have you noticed that the sun is shining this morning?—and that this is the first time it has shone in Lewis for ten days?" (This was a fact!)

"I regard that as a good omen. This is going to be a great meeting. This is going to be a friendly meeting. This meeting will mark the beginning of a new era in the history of this loyal island of Lewis that you love above all places on earth, and that I too have learned to love. So great is my regard for Lewis and its people that I am prepared to adventure a big sum of money for the development of the resources of the island and of the fisheries. Do you realise that Stornoway is right in the centre of the richest fishing grounds in the whole world? The fishing which has hitherto been carried on in an old-fashioned, happy-go-lucky way is now to be prosecuted on scientific lines. Recently at Stornoway I saw half of the fishing boats return to port without a single herring and the remainder with only a score of crans between them. That is a poor return for men who spend their time and risk their lives in a precarious calling [*ejaculations of assent*]. I have a plan for putting an end to that sort of thing [*the crowd is eagerly interested*].

"The fact is, your fishing as presently carried on is a hit or a miss. I want you to make it a hit every time. How can I do that? Well, every time you now put out to sea you blindly hope to strike a shoal of herrings. Sometimes you do. Oftener you do not. But the shoals are there if you only knew the spot—and *that* is where I can help you.

"I am prepared to supply a fleet of airplanes and trained observers who will daily scan the sea in circles round the island. An observer from one of these planes cannot fail to notice any shoal of herrings over which he passes

Immediately he does so he sends a wireless message to the Harbour Master at Stornoway. Every time a message of that kind comes in there is a 'loud-speaker' announcement by the Harbour Master so that all the skippers at the pier get the exact location of the shoal. The boats are headed for that spot—and next morning they steam back to port loaded with herrings to the gunwales. Hitherto, more often than not, the return to port has been with light boats and heavy hearts. In future it will be with light hearts and heavy boats! [*Loud cheers.*]

"I have already thought out plans which will involve me in an expenditure of five million pounds! But there has been some discord between us; we have not seen eye to eye. When two sensible people have a difference of opinion they do not quarrel: they meet and discuss their differences reasonably and calmly. This is what we have met for here to-day—and the sun is shining! But what do I propose to do with this five million pounds? Let me tell you." . . .

And then there appeared in the next few minutes the most graphic word-picture it is possible to imagine—a great fleet of fishing boats—another great fleet of cargo boats—a large fish-canning factory (already started)—railways—an electric-power station; then one could see the garden city grow—steady work, steady pay, beautiful houses for all—every modern convenience and comfort. The insecurity of their present income was referred to; the squalor of their present houses deftly compared with the conditions in the new earthly paradise. Altogether it was a masterpiece; and it produced its effect; little cheers came involuntarily from a few here and there—more cheers!—general cheers!! . . .

And just then, while the artist was still adding skilful detail, there was a dramatic interruption.

One of the ringleaders managed to rouse himself from the spell, and in an impassioned voice addressed the crowd in Gaelic, and this is what he said:

"*So so, fhiribh! Cha dean so gnothach! Bheireadh am bodach mil-bheulach sin chreidsinn oirnn gu'm bheil dubh geal 's geal dubh! Ciod e dhuinn na bruadairean briagha aige, a thig no nach tig? 'Se am fearann tha sinn ag iarraidh. Agus 'se tha mise a faighneachd* [turning to face Lord Leverhulme and pointing dramatically towards him]: *an toir thu dhuinn am fearann?*" The effect was electrical. The crowd roared their approbation.

Lord Leverhulme looked bewildered at this, to him, torrent of unintelligible sounds, but when the frenzied cheering with which it was greeted died down he spoke.

"I am sorry! It is my great misfortune that I do not understand the Gaelic language. But perhaps my interpreter will translate for me what has been said?"

Said the interpreter: "I am afraid, Lord Leverhulme, that it will be impossible for me to convey to you in English what has been so forcefully said in the older tongue; but I will do my best"—and his best was a masterpiece, not only in words but in tone and gesture and general effect:

"Come, come, men! This will not do! This honey-mouthed man would have us believe that black is white and white is black. *We* are not concerned with his fancy dreams that may or may not come true! What we want is the *land*—and the question I put to him now is: *will you give us the land?* "

The translation evoked a further round of cheering. A voice was heard to say:

"Not so bad for a poor language like the English!"

Lord Leverhulme's picture, so skilfully painted, was spattered in the artist's hand!

But was it? When the cheering died down the brave

little artist looked round the crowd with eyes that seemed to pierce every separate individual. Finally he fixed a cold-steel look on the interrupter and in a clean-cut staccato accent said:

"You have asked a straight question. I like a straight question; and I like a straight answer. And my answer to your question is 'NO.' I am *not* prepared to give you the land" (here a compelling hand-wave that instantly silenced some protests), "not because I am vindictively opposed to your views and aspirations, but because I conscientiously believe that if my views are listened to— if my schemes are given a chance—the result will be enhanced prosperity and greater happiness for Lewis and its people. Listen." . . . And the indomitable little artist took up his work again in such skilful fashion that in a matter of seconds he had the ear and the eye of the crowd again—and in five minutes they were cheering him again. . . . Theatre! Play!

But the play was not yet over. A clean-shaven æsthete —a crofter-fisherman—cut in politely at a momentary pause in the artist's work. He spoke slowly, in English, with a strong Lewis accent; each word set square like a stone block in a building, and he made a great speech.

"Lord Leverhulme," said he, "will you allow me to intervene in this debate for a few moments?" (Assent signified.) "Thank you. Well, I will begin by saying that we give credit to your lordship for good *intentions* in this matter. We believe you *think* you are *right*, but we *know* that you are *wrong*. The fact is, there is an element of sentiment in the situation which it is impossible for your lordship to understand. But for that we do not blame you; it is not your *fault* but your *misfortune* that your upbringing, your experience, and your outlook are such that a proper understanding of the position and of our point of view is quite outwith your comprehension.

You have spoken of steady work and steady pay in tones of veneration—and I have no doubt that in your view, and in the view of those unfortunate people who are compelled to live their lives in smoky towns, steady work and steady pay are very desirable things. But in Lewis we have never been accustomed to either—and, strange though it must seem to your lordship, *we do not greatly desire them*. We attend to our crofts in seed-time and harvest, and we follow the fishing in its season—and when neither requires our attention we are free to *rest and contemplate*. You have referred to our houses as hovels—but they are our *homes*, and I will venture to say, my lord, that, poor though these homes may be, you will find more *real human happiness* in them than you will find in your *castles* throughout the land. I would impress on you that we are not in opposition to your schemes of work; we only oppose you when you say you *cannot give us the land*, and on that point we will oppose you with all our strength. It may be that some of the younger and less thoughtful men will side with you, but believe me, the great majority of us are against you.

"Lord Leverhulme! You have bought this island. But you have not bought *us*, and we refuse to be the bond-slaves of any man. We want to live our own lives in our own way, poor in material things it may be, but at least it will be clear of the fear of the factory bell; it will be *free and independent*!"

After a short silence of astonishment there came the loudest and longest cheers of that day. "That's the way to talk, lad!" "That's yourself, boy," and such like encomiums were shouted from all quarters. One voice demanded to know what "Bodach an t-siapuinn" [1] could say to that? Nobody thought he could say anything to that: the enemy was annihilated!

[1] The wee soap-mannie.

But we had yet to grasp the full fighting qualities of this wonderful little man, and we were soon to see him in action, at his very best. With a sort of magical combination of hand and eye he again commanded a perfect silence; he then spoke in modulated, cajoling tones that showed the superb actor.

Said he: "Will you allow me to congratulate you?—to thank you for putting the views of my opponents so clearly before me? I did know that sentiment lay at the back of the opposition to my schemes, but I confess I had not adequately estimated the strength of that element till now. My friends! sentiment is the finest thing in this hard world. It is the golden band of brotherhood. It is the beautiful mystic thing that makes life worth living . . . and would you accuse me of deliberately planning to injure that beautiful thing? No! No! A thousand times No! Then is there, after all, so very much between your point of view and mine? Are we not striving after the same thing?—by different roads it may be, but still, for the same goal? We are both out for the greatest good of the greatest number of people on this island. You have admitted, that the *young men* may believe in my schemes. May I again congratulate you? The young people will—and do—believe in my schemes. I have in my pocket now (fetching out a handful of letters) quite a number of letters from young men in different parts of the island, and I have received a great many more of the same kind—all asking the same questions— 'When can you give me a job in Stornoway?' 'When can I get one of your new houses?' These young men and their wives and sweethearts want to give up the croft life; they want a brighter, happier life. . . . My friends! the young people of to-day will be *the* people of to-morrow. Are the older ones who have had their day going to stand in the way of the young folk? Are we older fellows going to be dogs-in-mangers? No! The people of this island are much too intelligent to take up so un-Christian an attitude. Give me a chance—give my schemes a chance —give the young folks and give Lewis a chance! Give me a period of ten years to develop my schemes and I venture to prophesy that long before then—in fact in the near future—so many people, young and old, will believe in them, that crofts will be going a-begging—and then if there are still some who prefer life on the land they can have two, three, four crofts apiece!"

And the crowd cheered again: they simply could not resist it, and they cheered loud and long.

The artist knew when to stop. As the cheers died he raised his hat and said: "Ladies and Gentlemen— *Friends*—I knew the sun did not shine for nothing! This has been a great meeting. This will be a memorable day in the history of Lewis. You are giving me a chance. I will not fail you. I thank you. Good day." And off he walked to another round of cheering.

I tried to walk off too—unsuccessfully. An eager crowd surged round "the man from the Board": "When will the Board be dividing off the land?"

"You do not want the land now," said I, well knowing they did, notwithstanding the cheers.

"Want the land! Of course we want the land, and we want it at once."

"But you gave Lord Leverhulme the impression that you agreed with him," said I, affecting astonishment.

"Not at all," was the reply, "and if he is under that impression you may tell him from us that he is greatly mistaken."

"But why did you cheer him?" I inquired.

"Och! well: he made a very good speech and he is a very clever man, and we wanted to show our appreciation

—but the land is another matter"—and that, I knew, was the real position.

When I joined Lord Leverhulme later in a near-by shooting lodge he was in great form, and it was with keen regret that I began the task of disillusioning him. At first he was incredulous. He could not understand what he called such "double dealing." I tried to explain and let both sides down gently. When he realised the truth he became very downcast. But after a few minutes he brightened up and said: "Anyhow, that was a great meeting! They are an intelligent people, and I never give up hope so long as I have an intelligent opposition to deal with. Besides, there is not the same enjoyment in things that are easily won. I am enjoying this fight and I shall win them over yet!"

"I am very sorry," said I, "to have to resort again to the cold-water jug, but if you could see the position as I see it you would be less optimistic—unless you are prepared to compromise on the question of the land, which I venture to think you could do without material hurt to your schemes."

"I shall *not* compromise," he retorted with emphasis, "and as for optimism, I have always been an optimist. I am like the Irishman who fell from the roof of a New York skyscraper. His friend working at a window lower down yelled as Pat shot past: 'Hello, Pat! Are yez all roight?' 'Yes, bejabbers,' shouted Pat, 'so far!'"

CHAPTER XXIV

Dinner at the Castle

Soon after arriving in Lewis—to play so inglorious a part in the Leverhulme *v.* Natives clash—I called to see my friend the late Duncan MacKenzie of the Royal Hotel. It was always good policy to "get the breath" of that remarkable man on any question affecting the island. In half an hour I was well posted in the present state of the campaign, coloured with piquant side-lights on the disposition of the fighting forces of the two sides.

Dinners and dances at the Castle were in the forefront of Lord Leverhulme's strategy. There were several such per week, and nearly every person of influence sooner or later found himself—and his wife or daughter—at one of these delightful banquets.

"You'll be at a dinner at the Castle within the week," was Duncan's jocular prophecy.

He was right; and when the invitation came I could not suppress a smile. It was after the meeting at the farm described in the last chapter.

After the joke about the optimistic Irishman, Lord Leverhulme left the subject of the land and switched on to another.

"By the way," he inquired, "have you got any special engagement for this evening?"

It was then I smiled at the recollection of Duncan MacKenzie's prophecy; and before I could reply he added:

"I'll tell you why I ask. I am having a few friends to dinner at the Castle to-night and would be delighted if you could come."

"Thanks very much," I said, "but no! no! I'm not in the habit of dining with lords in castles!"

"You mean clothes?" said he. "Never mind about clothes! Come just as you like—so long as you don't come in pyjamas!"

"Right then!" I decided. "I'll be there."

"Good! My car will call for you at seven-thirty."

There was a big dinner-party and Lord Leverhulme was the ideal host who manages to give each guest the impression that he or she is someone just a little special. His "management" of the mixed elements in the party was a masterpiece. He seemed to exercise a sort of mesmeric power over his guests, that bent them readily but unconsciously to his will. Soon I felt I would have no will of my own at all, so potent was this influence. I was seated next but one to him. In a crude effort to retain a remnant of my individuality I challenged facetiously:

"Are you aware, Lord Leverhulme, that you are committing a breach of Highland etiquette?"

"Really?" he inquired. "And what is my crime?"

"I have been waiting for a lead from you with the bottle," I explained.

"I *am* so sorry," he jokingly apologised; and then, in the oracular manner which he readily affected, he proceeded: "Whisky is uncertain in its effects. It affects different people differently. Some of my friends who are ordinarily rather dull fellows become quite inspired by a glass or two of Scotch. They become eloquent, witty; they seem to think more clearly and quickly. Now if I were to take even the tiniest drop of whisky it would have the opposite effect. It would make me witless; my thinking would be confused. I cannot afford to let my thoughts get confused; so I do not take any whisky. But, please . . . please . . . !"

"Thank you," I said; "and I hope I may rank with some of your friends!"

How skilfully and unobtrusively that Bodachan dominated the situation from his chair at the top of the table; and later with equal skill and urbanity directed the social activities of the evening! There was music, dancing, and some very good singing—in English and Gaelic—and much merriment. At one stage a few of the young girls called for a song from Lord Leverhulme.

"Ladies! Ladies!" he protested. "You *know* I cannot sing. I just croak!"

But the lassies jingo-ringed him, chanting:

> "Lord Leverhulme for the Bathing song,
> Lord Leverhulme for the Bathing song!"

He pretended to be shocked: "That dreadful song!" But the insistent chant continued. Then with dramatic suddenness he agreed.

"Very well! If you insist I shall sing a song—and I shall sing the Bathing song."

It was quite true: he couldn't sing: he could only croak; and that versatile little man croaked heartily through a song which would make an Irish navvy blush. As encore, in the Lancashire dialect, he gave an excellent recitation displaying real humour and histrionic ability of a high order.

Soon after the recitation, when everything was going noisily and merrily, I felt a firm grip on my bicep and a quiet voice said in my ear:

"Let us go over to a quiet place behind the pillars. I want to have a word with you."

My hour had come!

We seated ourselves in a quiet corner. Not a trace of gaiety now on that alert countenance. His eyes fixed me with a "now-to-business" sort of look which must have stood him in good stead in many a tussle. His speech was as direct as his look. Perforce I adopted a similar manner and this is a fairly accurate record of our conversation:

L.L. "I should like to know exactly how I stand with you. Are you with me or against me?"

ME. "You mean: 'Do I think the Board will be with or against your schemes?'"

L.L. "Put it that way if you like, but please, *please* do not be evasive. You know, and you know that I know, that the Board will be largely guided by you in this matter. Are—you—with—me—or—against—me?"

ME. "I do not yet know. I have not made up my mind. I see both sides. You see only one. Tell me this. You said to-day at the meeting that you had arranged to spend five million pounds on your development schemes here. I cannot quite grasp what even one million means, but at least I have an idea that five million pounds is a lot of money. Do you expect to get a return from that expenditure?—and how?"

L.L. (*registering horror*). "I am not a philanthropist in this matter! I would not put a penny into this venture if I did not see that it would be a commercial success. Never have I seen the successful end of a venture so clearly as I do now. Not that I require—or desire—to make more money for myself. I am never sure on a given day just what I am worth in money, but last time my accountant reported to me it was in the neighbourhood of eighteen million pounds. In any case I have more money than I can possibly require. But I derive my greatest pleasure in life from business ventures which call for thought and vision. That is a great game: the creation of wealth— and thereby providing steady work and good wages for thousands of people."

ME. "I can understand that; but what on earth is

there in this rather barren island that offers economic scope for so huge a capital expenditure?"

L.L. "You appear to be intelligent. You probably are. But *vision* is also required here. You know this island. Did you know that, if you take a map, fix one leg of a pair of compasses in the town of Stornoway and describe a circle of a hundred miles radius, within that circle *you have the richest fishing grounds in the whole world* ?"

ME. "No. I did not."

L.L. "Quite. Well, you have. That is a very important fact. Fish is a valuable human food. That is also important. How can I link up these terminal facts? I shall create the necessary connecting links so that I shall have a chain leading from the bed of the Minch to the breakfast-tables of the world. First I must catch my fish. I shall soon have the best and the best-equipped fishing fleet the world has ever seen.

"My fish must be conveyed quickly to the railheads. I shall have a fleet of fast carrier-boats for that.

"I am in process of acquiring so substantial a block of railway company shares that there will be no fear of my fish rotting at the sidings!

"I am getting on! But am I going to incur all this expense and risk, and then allow another fellow to reap the reward? No! I have already purchased most of the biggest retail fish-shops in the big consuming centres. My fish will be sold in *my* shops.

"But I shall catch more fish than I can sell *fresh*. Well, I shall can the surplus. I have built what I believe to be the most up-to-date fish-canning factory in existence. I know little of the process of canning but I pay an expert from Norway two thousand pounds a year to advise me.

"I shall make my own cans—and I shall make my own labels. Labels are very important. I have recently had submitted to me various label designs. Some are from men who put R.A. or A.R.A. after their names. I have made my selection. It has red lettering on a white ground. The letters spell

LEWIS CANNED FISH

This is printed in slanting fashion three times in the full round of the can.

"I have placed a can with that label inside a window of the Castle. I have looked at it from every angle and from just outside the window and from twenty yards away. It strikes me in the eye from every angle and from every distance. I cannot escape it!

"Canned fish is like whisky: the longer you keep it (up to a point) the better it gets. When my first 'cure' is properly matured I send a consignment to my principal corner shops with instructions to make a good window display on the Saturday.

"John Smith has been busy in the office all the week (or so he tells the wife) and late home every night. On Saturday he goes home to lunch. Conscience-stricken he tries to make amends.

"'Mary, my dear,' says he, 'you've had a dreary week of it. What about a show to-night?'

"Poor Mary is overjoyed. What a considerate man is her John! On the way to the theatre they are held up at the corner for a car—the corner where my shop is. The light from the window shows up LEWIS CANNED FISH most attractively. It catches Mary's eye.

"'I say, John, what a lovely label! Lewis Canned Fish. I like the look of it. . . . Just a minute. . . .'

"'What is this Lewis Canned Fish?' she asks.

"'Madam,' says my salesman. 'It *is* Lewis Canned Fish and very delightful too.'

"'Can you recommend it?'

"'Thoroughly, madam. I believe it is the best canned fish in the world.'

"'Thank you. Will you please send along a tin?'

"Back from the show Mary is peckish. That can just asks to be opened. They have Lewis Canned Fish for supper. They have never tasted anything so good. *They lick their fingers*. Nyum nyum!

"Monday morning Mrs Smith is in the back green hanging up the washing. Mrs Brown is over the wall on the right.

"'Mrs Brown! Do you know! I made the most *wonderful* discovery on Saturday!'—and she lets Mrs Brown into the secret. She also tells Mrs Jones on the left. Each buys a can. . . .

"And so the great news spreads and spreads. Within a year—certainly within two years—there is *only one canned fish that counts in the world*, and that is LEWIS CANNED FISH."

It is impossible to convey in mere writing the force, the eloquence, the abounding self-assurance that radiated from this visionary as he expounded his plans. He was as an evangelist preaching a gospel. He all but mesmerised me. It needed a real effort to hang on to the one thing I knew to be true—namely, that nothing at that time could effectively stand between the returned Lewis soldiers and sailors and their land.

"Almost thou persuadest me," I quoted, "and I thank you for paying me the compliment of giving me a glimpse of your business methods. Now I understand how your various ventures have been so successful.

"But, Lord Leverhulme, however much you may convince me that you would be equally successful in Lewis it would but mislead you if I said I thought you could convince Lewis men of that. Certainly nothing you can promise them will induce them to drop their demand for crofts. But surely there is a middle way. The retention of the large farms is not essential to the success of your schemes."

"I need them for the production of milk for supplying the greatly increased population which will be one of the direct results of my schemes," he rapped at me.

"You can import milk from the mainland," I countered. "That is being done now—and better and cheaper milk than you can produce in Lewis."

"My agricultural expert advises me I must have the farms. In this matter I must be guided by him."

"I do not question the ability of your agricultural expert to advise you—in England. But—with respect— Lewis is not England."

"But I *must* have control of my factory hands! How can I have that in the case of men who are in the independent position of crofters?"

"That is just the point," I urged. "That is what was made so clear at the meeting to-day. These men will not tolerate being subject to your whim or charity. But if you initiate friendly relationships by giving them crofts you will have no lack of men willing to work in your factories. By opposing their desire you will but stimulate their opposition and in the end they will beat you. In one word my advice is—*compromise.*"

"I will *not* compromise. I *must* control," he reiterated again and again.

"Then I am afraid you are only at the beginning of your troubles," I sighed; "but at least I sincerely wish you good luck—and no one will be more pleased than I if I should prove a poor prophet."

After events in Lewis proved Lord Leverhulme's optimism to have been no better founded than Pat's. His failure to understand and meet the views of the people led to the failure of all his projects. A little mutual compromise would have enabled both sides to attain, substantially, their particular ambitions. But Lord Leverhulme refused to compromise until towards the very end—and then it was too late. Farm after farm had to be broken up until at last he abandoned the whole venture and left the island—never to return.

Is that a matter for regret? Or is it not? I cannot say. I have merely tried to tell the story of the most interesting incident in my official experience.

JOURNEY ENDING

The Journey is nearing its end. This book gives but a sketchy glimpse of a few of its incidents. How, as a whole, has it gone? Listen—

Lerwick of the Silver Horde, North Isles, Muckle Flugga, Fitful Head—

Pomona, Stones of Stennes, Old Man of Hoy, Ola of the dreaded Firth—

Stacks of Duncansby, Dunnet Head, Deil's Brig and fearful Clett—

Ben Hope and Loyal, Cape Wrath of the angry waters, Canisp, Suilven—

Summer Isles, Lochmaree, Slioch, Ben Wyvis (*mo ghaol!*)—

Dunvegan, Duntulm, Fairy Bridge—and the snowclad peaks of Cuchuilein cutting the crimson of a winter's sunrise—

Loch Duich and the Sisters of Kintail—

Lochaber of the wild men and strong, Glen Finnan, Sands of Morar—

Glen of Weeping, Buachaille Etive, Ben Dòrain of the song—

Mull of the mountains, Coll and Tiree of rich pastures—

And then? And then! Behold the Hebrides! Enchanted Islands of the West! Sanctuary of soul-rest and heart-healing where time is properly regarded as the infinite thing it is; whose spell, once cast, is ever potent. Islands of bent-grass and seaweed, of salmon and sea-trout, of wild wheeling greylag, of curlew and teal; of song and of story, of Gaelic and homespun, of peat-fires so radiant, of hearts warm and leal :

> Muran 's Feamainn,
> Cladach 's Tràigh,
> Machair 's Mointeach,
> Céilidh 's Ceòl;
>
> Giomach 's Gealag,
> Liathag 's Leòbag,
> Glas-gheadh cho fiadhaich,
> Muinntir cho còir!

Truly, the Journey has been along a delightful road.

Some Books published by

THE MORAY PRESS, 21 George Street, Edinburgh

HELEN DREVER.

THE LURE OF THE KELPIE and Other Tales and Legends.
Illustrated by Mildred R. Lamb. A selection of the best fairy tales
from the Mainland and Isles of the Highlands.   **6s.** (Postage **4d.**)

TALES OF THE SCOTTISH CLANS. Illustrated by Mason
Trotter.   **6s.** (Postage **4d.**)

THOMAS HENDERSON.

A SCOTS GARLAND. An Anthology of Scottish Vernacular Verse.
With etched Title-page and Frontispiece.   **5s.** (Postage **3d.**)

THE FINDHORN : THE RIVER OF BEAUTY.   Illustrated with
drawings.   **7s. 6d.** (Postage **6d.**)

DONALD A. MACCULLOCH.

ROMANTIC LOCHABER.   Illustrated   from   the   Author's
Photographs.   **10s. 6d.** (Postage **7d.**)

ALISTAIR MACLEAN.

HEBRIDEAN ALTARS. Translations of prayers and runes
collected throughout the Hebrides from the original Gaelic.
                                   6s. (Postage **4d.**)

AMY MURRAY.

FATHER ALLAN'S ISLAND. Island lore and folk-song gathered
in Eriskay.   With music.   **6s.** (Postage **6d.**)

DAVID RORIE.

THE LUM HAT WANTIN' THE CROON.   A new and enlarged
edition of Dr Rorie's well-known book, *The Auld Doctor.*
                                   5s. (Postage **4d.**)

J. B. SALMOND.

WADE IN SCOTLAND. An historical and topographical study
of Wade's Roads.   Fully illustrated.   **5s.** (Postage **6d.**)

THE OLD STALKER AND OTHER VERSES. **5s.** (Postage **3d.**)

CATHERINE P. SLATER.

MARGET POW. A famous Scots character study full of subtle
humour and practical philosophy. With a frontispiece in four
colours by H. W. Kerr, R.S.A.   **5s.** (Postage **4d.**)